HIKE
THE REDWOODS

Hike. Contemplate what makes you happy and what makes you happier still. Follow a trail or blaze a new one. **Hike.** Think about what you can do to expand your life and someone else's. **Hike.** Slow down. Gear up. **Hike.** Connect with friends. Re-connect with nature.

Hike. Shed stress. Feel blessed. **Hike** to remember. **Hike** to forget. **Hike** for recovery. **Hike** for discovery. **Hike.** Enjoy the beauty of providence. **Hike.** Share the way, The Hiker's Way, on the long and winding trail we call life.

HIKE
THE REDWOODS

BY

JOHN MCKINNEY

TheTrailmaster.com

HIKE the Redwoods, Best Day Hikes in Redwood National and State Parks by John McKinney

HIKE the Redwoods ©2022 The Trailmaster, Inc.

Book Design by Lisa DeSpain
Cartography by Mark Chumley
HIKE Series Editor: Cheri Rae

Published by Olympus Press and The Trailmaster, Inc.
TheTrailmaster.com (Visit our site for a complete listing of all Trailmaster publications, products, and services.)

Although The Trailmaster, Inc. and the author have made every attempt to ensure that information in this book is accurate, they are not responsible for any loss, damage, injury, or inconvenience that may occur to you while using this information. You are responsible for your own safety; the fact that an activity or trail is described in this book does not mean it will be safe for you. Trail conditions can change from day to day; always check local conditions and know your limitations.

CONTENTS

INTRODUCTION 9

REDWOOD NATIONAL AND STATE PARKS 15

Southern Redwood NP Near Visitor Center

REDWOOD CREEK 25
Short hike or overnight backpack through the heart of
the national park.

TALL TREES GROVE 29
Pick up a permit and hit the trail to the Howard
Libbey Tree, once considered the tallest redwood.

DOLASON PRAIRIE 33
Tall grasses and tall trees, wildflower-splashed
meadows and ocean views.

LADY BIRD JOHNSON GROVE 37
Hike an engaging nature trail and find out where
Redwood National Park was dedicated—and why.

BERRY GLEN 41
From Elk Meadow to Lady Bird Johnson Grove with
plenty of redwoods along the way.

TRILLIUM FALLS 45
Loop amidst old growth and North Coast's iconic
wildflower.

LOST MAN CREEK 49
Find a lovely creek, rocky pools and a lush forest.

Prairie Creek Redwoods State Park

CATHEDRAL TREES...53
  Big Tree and splendid congregations of redwoods on a
  feature-packed little loop.

MINERS RIDGE..57
  Hike classic James Irvine Trail and two more trails to
  Godwood Creek and grand groves.

WEST RIDGE & PRAIRIE CREEK...................................61
  Premiere paths lead to dense redwood groves and a
  fern-filled, redwood cloaked ridge. Great vistas, too!

BROWN CREEK...65
  Trio of trails visit a magical forest of mighty redwoods
  and colorful rhodendrons.

SKUNK CABBAGE CREEK...69
  From slopes of moss-draped Sitka spruce and skunk
  cabbage to Gold Bluffs beach.

FERN CANYON...73
  Many "fern canyons" thrive in the redwoods; this is
  undoubtedly the most awe-inspiring.

GOLD BLUFFS BEACH..77
  Primo length of coastal trail leads to trio of waterfalls
  and the odd Ossagon Rocks.

CARRUTHERS COVE..81
  Descend from cliff-tops to sea stacks and walk a wild
  beach.

Northern Redwood NP and
Del Norte Coast Redwoods SP

FLINT RIDGE...87
  Ramble Coastal Trail over redwood dotted ridge for
  vistas of the Klamath River.

HIDDEN BEACH & REQUA OVERLOOK 91
Coastal Trail leads from lagoon to Sitka spruce forest
to Klamath River vistas.

DAMNATION CREEK 95
Steep trail plunges from redwood forest to the sea with
Pacific vistas along the way.

OLD COAST HIGHWAY 99
Hike to Enderts Beach and beyond on Coastal
Highway that's now Coastal Trail.

Jedediah Smith Redwoods State Park

BOY SCOUT TREE & FERN FALL 105
Boy Scout Trail travels through the heart of Jedediah
Smith Redwoods State Park.

STOUT GROVE 109
Is it "The World's Most Scenic Grove of Redwoods?"
You be the judge.

GROVE OF TITANS 113
Mill Creek Trail and a new elevated boardwalk lead to
the Del Norte Titan and a grove of giant redwoods.

SMITH RIVER 119
Head out on Hiouchi Trail along the redwood
forested-bluffs above California's wildest river.

REDWOOD STORIES 114

CALIFORNIA'S NATIONAL PARKS 130

ABOUT THE AUTHOR 142

Contemplate the redwoods and remember the
words of Buddha: "If you are facing in the right
direction, all you need to do is keep on the trail."

EVERY TRAIL TELLS A STORY.

INTRODUCTION

Nature's wonders are many: fern-filled canyons, 40 miles of wild coast and the tallest trees on earth.

National park visitors are few: the redwoods are rarely crowded, even at the height of the summer tourist season.

And the hiking is great: a superb network of trails leads to and through the redwoods, some groves easy-to-reach, others a half-day's walk away.

Redwood National and State Parks protect about 45 percent of the remaining coast redwoods. The national park and three state parks (Jedediah Smith Coast Redwoods, Del Norte Coast Redwoods and Prairie Creek Redwoods) are caretakers of the Howard Libbey Tree in Tall Trees Grove, Del Norte Titan in Grove of the Titans, and Hyperion (#1 at 379.7 feet) in a remote region of Redwood National Park.

Something in our human nature is drawn to the superlative—the oldest, deepest and, in this case the highest—and visitors from across the nation and around the world are drawn to the redwoods by their stature. But there's more to the redwoods than their height, and more to a redwood forest than trees, however high they reach to the sky.

Dim and quiet, wrapped in mist and silence, the redwoods roof a moist and mysterious world. Entering this special world, meandering over lush ground and inhaling the fragrance of wood and water is a glorious, even spiritual experience.

Any fan of ferns will love hiking through the redwoods. Oh, those tall sword ferns at Stout Grove! Fern Canyon in Prairie Creek Redwoods State Park is the most awe-inspiring of the many beautiful "fern canyons" found along the North Coast. Bracken, five-finger, lady, sword, and chain ferns smother the precipitous walls of the canyon.

Another highlight of hiking the redwoods is traipsing through the lush undergrowth. California huckleberry, azalea, mosses, lichen, and five-fingered ferns are everywhere—springing out of logs and stumps in a wild and dazzling profusion that you might associate with the Amazon.

Lucky hikers might catch a glimpse of the herd of Roosevelt elk that roam Prairie Creek Redwoods State Park. These graceful animals look like a cross between a South American llama and a deer, and may even convince (if any convincing be necessary) hikers that they have indeed entered an enchanted land.

The redwoods first draw us to RNSP, but often it's the region's spectacular coast that prompts a return visit. Dramatic bluffs, hidden coves, tide pools, and wilderness beaches are linked by a 40-mile length of the California Coastal Trail. The trail offers splendid day hiking and backpacking opportunities.

As you hike the redwoods, you might pick up a distinct redwood forest vocabulary—colorful words and terms from "albino redwood" to "widow-maker." My favorite is "Cathedral Trees," groups of trees that have grown up from the living remains of the stump of a fallen redwood; because they grew from the perimeter of a round stump, they are arranged in a circle.

Where the best hikes are has a lot to do with where the best trees are. Timber companies cut the most accessible redwoods first, the most inaccessible redwoods last. Remaining old-growth groves and forests are often remote and isolated from one another—in different watersheds, different parklands and located many miles apart.

That being said, US 101, aka the Redwood Highway, extends the length of the RNSP and most of the trailheads for hikes into the redwood forest or along the redwood coast can be accessed from well-marked pullouts, roads and exits from 101.

Redwood parks and trails are open year-round. Most visitors travel to the redwoods in the summer and find a warm welcome in the form of helpful summer staff in five visitor centers.

Park staff installs summer-only footbridges that make it possible to cross creeks and rivers. Examples include a bridge over Mill Creek near Stout Grove and several bridges over Redwood Creek. These bridges bestow big benefits: hikers get to keep their boots dry; they offer great places for contemplation and photo ops; they help hikers make loop trips that otherwise would be much more difficult without safe crossing of what are sometimes powerful watercourses.

The unique topography and climate of the North Coast prompt the growth of REALLY BIG Trees.

One of the best times for a hike is in late spring when the rains (usually) stop and the rhododendrons are blooming, pink and conspicuous beneath the tall trees. Other seasonal highlights include bird migrations in spring and fall. Look for displays of fall color from the maples and other deciduous trees.

In winter, it can rain and rain and rain in redwood country. Actually, the rainy season can extend from October through April! Nevertheless, for the well-prepared hiker, a rainy day hike in the redwoods is a memorable experience indeed, and I highly recommend it.

Hike smart, reconnect with nature and have a wonderful time in the redwoods.

Hike on.

—John McKinney

Looking it over: RNSP is a collection of parklands located along the coast in Humboldt and Del Norte counties.

EVERY TRAIL TELLS A STORY.

REDWOOD NATIONAL PARK

Geography

Located along the coast in far northern California, Redwoods National and State Parks includes the National Park created in 1968 and a trio of state park—Jedediah Smith Redwoods State Park, Del Norte Redwoods State Park and Prairie Creek Redwoods State Park. Collectively the parks (131,983 acres) protect about 45 percent of the remaining coast redwoods.

RNSP is located near the northern limit of the coast redwoods' narrow range. Even during the summer, fog and cool ocean breezes serve to keep the redwoods damp. Eureka, gateway to RNSP, and its neighboring city of Arcata are the only two cities on the West Coast of the U.S. where the temperature has never exceeded 90 degrees.

Rivers, known for their salmon and steelhead fishing and for their great beauty, are a major feature in RNSP. The Smith River, California's last major free-flowing river flows from the Siskiyou Mountains through the parks' north section. The Klamath River crosses the middle of the parkland and Redwood Creek runs through the southern portion.

RNSP is not one contiguous park but rather a collection of parklands located inland and along the coast in Humboldt and Del Norte counties. The parks are linked south to north by Highway 101(aka the Redwood Highway) which extends along the north coast to its junction with Highway 199 near Crescent City.

Northern spotted owl, resident species of old-growth redwood forests

Natural History

With just the right combination of moisture, climate, elevation and longitude, California's northern coast provides the only environment in the world where redwoods thrive. Redwoods were around during the age of dinosaurs in the Jurassic Era 160 million years ago and have occupied their present range for some 20 million years.

So far the tallest (reported) tree is the Hyperion (379 feet 4 inches), growing in a remote and undisclosed location in RNSP. Many believe taller trees await discovery.

Along with the redwoods, Douglas fir, Sitka spruce, tanoak, madrone, big-leaf maple, California laurel and red alder are commonly found in the

Bachelor Party: Bull Roosevelt congregate on the grasslands of Prairie Creek Redwoods SP.

forest. Redwood forest understory includes California rhododendron and azalea, prolific sword ferns, carpets of redwood sorrel, huckleberry and blackberry.

Most people know RNSP as home to the tallest trees on Earth, but the parks also protect a diversity of habitats. The Smith River, Klamath River, Redwood Creek and smaller creeks provide freshwater environments. Grassy prairies are important parts of the park mosaic and provide crucial habitat for wildlife including rabbits, black-tailed deer and the iconic Roosevelt elk.

The RNSP coast has a great diversity of wildlife, including bird species, fish, and tide pool inhabitants. From the Coastal Trail, hikers may spot harbor seals, California sea lions and Pacific gray whales.

In recognition of the rare ecosystem of the redwoods protected in RNSP, the United Nations designated it a World Heritage Site 1980 and an International Biosphere in 1983.

RNSP protects numerous threatened species including the bald eagle, Northern spotted owl, brown pelican, Chinook salmon and Stellers Sea Lion.

Along with its splendid tall tree sanctuaries, RNSP also includes a lot of logged land undergoing serious rehab. Miles of tractor trails and logging roads, which turn into stream channels and cause terrible erosion during winter rains, are being removed, land re-contoured, hillsides replanted. Restoring the ancient forest is a process that takes a very, very long time.

Conservation History

In the mid-19th century, more than 2 million acres of redwood forest flourished along the California coast. After decades of unregulated logging, much of it particularly destructive clear-cutting, the Save the Redwoods League was founded and effective conservation efforts began in the 1920s. As a result, numerous groves and state parks were preserved.

The discovery of "the world's tallest tree" by a 1963 National Geographic expedition provided impetus for the creation of a national park. The 367-foot high redwood and the ancient giants around it served as the rallying point for conservationists.

Amidst much controversy, Congress approved park legislation in 1968 and President Lyndon Johnson signed into law the bill creating 58,000-acre Redwood National Park.

"Save the redwoods!" was mission of ardent conservationists in the 1920s.

By the time the park was formed, nearly 90% of California's original old-growth redwood trees had been logged.

Many more redwoods were cut down before the park was expanded in 1978. In 1994, the National Park Service and California State Parks agreed to combine to administer the redwoods in the region to better manage the forest and watersheds as well as to provide recreation and visitor services.

Irony in the forest: President Richard Nixon dedicated a grove to Lady Bird Johnson, wife of his longtime political rival Lyndon B. Johnson.

Visitor Information

Redwood National and State Parks headquarters and Crescent City Information Center are located at 1111 Second Street in Crescent City. The center has exhibits and a bookstore and is open daily 9 am to 5 pm (winter to 4 pm). For more information, call 707-465-7335 or visit nps.gov/redw/

Thomas H. Kuchel Visitor Center (open daily 9 am to 5 pm/ 4pm winter), located off US Highway 101 near Orick, is the main visitor center for RNSP with exhibits and a bookstore, as well as guided talks and walks and beach access. For more information call 707-465-7765.

Summer-only information centers include Hiouchi Information Center (707-458-3294), northern gateway to RNSP, located off Highway 199 and Jedediah Smith Visitor Center (707-458-3496) located in Jedediah Smith Redwoods State Park. Beyond the summer season, staffing hours vary for Prairie Creek Visitor Center (707-488-2171), located in Prairie Creek Redwoods State Park.

For help locating restaurants and lodging for your travels to Redwood National Park, call the Del Norte Chamber of Commerce 719-657-9081 or visit visitdelnortecounty.com.

*Follow the fog belt to find the coastal redwoods,
like these in Lady Bird Johnson Grove.*

EVERY TRAIL TELLS A STORY.

I
SOUTHERN
REDWOOD NP

HIKE ON.

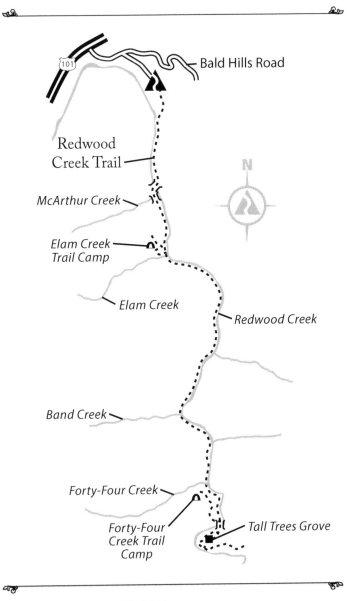

Bald Hills Road

Redwood
Creek Trail

McArthur Creek

Elam Creek
Trail Camp

Elam Creek

Redwood Creek

Band Creek

Forty-Four Creek

Forty-Four
Creek Trail
Camp

Tall Trees Grove

N

101

TheTrailmaster.com

REDWOOD CREEK

REDWOOD CREEK TRAIL

To first creek crossing is 3.2 miles round trip; to Tall Trees Grove is 8.3 miles one way with 500-foot elevation gain

Redwood Creek Trail travels through the heart of the national park to Tall Trees Grove, site of (what was once considered) the world's tallest measured tree. After one of the classic conservation battles of the 1960s, a narrow corridor of land along Redwood Creek was acquired to protect a giant coast redwood (367.8 feet).

The 9-mile stretch along Redwood Creek, once known as "the worm" was down-slope from private timberlands, where extensive clear-cut logging took place. Resulting slope erosion and stream sediments threatened the big trees; in order to protect this watershed, the NPS purchased additional acreage in Redwood Creek basin.

Redwood Creek Trail makes a gentle ascent from the outskirts of Orick to Tall Trees Grove. The three bridges that cross Redwood Creek are in place only during the summer. Inquire at the visitor center before attempting this hike during the wetter seasons.

Opt for an easy walk amidst red alder and big-leaf maple along the banks of the creek to the first (summer) bridge crossing, a strenuous round trip day hike or a pleasant backpack. Get a free permit for camping along this trail at Redwood Information Center.

DIRECTIONS: From Highway 101, about 2 miles north of Orick, turn east on Bald Hills Road. Take the first right and drive 0.5 mile to parking and the Redwood Creek trailhead.

THE HIKE: The trail passes through regenerating forest of red alder as well as old growth Sitka spruce and redwood. Elk are frequently observed in the lovely meadows flanking Redwood Creek.

About 1.5 miles from the trailhead, the path reaches the first bridge crossing of Redwood Creek. Continue south, pausing at occasional clearings to get the "big picture" of Redwood Creek.

As the trail meanders with the creek, three distinct communities of flora can be discerned. Extensive grass prairie, emerald green during the wet season and golden brown during the drier months, dominates the eastern slopes above Redwood Creek. Down-slope of the grassland are vast clearcuts, slowly recovering as new-growth red alder forest. Near the creek are the groves of old growth redwoods and a lush understory of salmonberry, redwood sorrel and sword fern.

During the summer, the hiker may descend to Redwood Creek and travel the creek's gravel bars nearly to Tall Trees Grove. The river bars are fine pathways and also serve as campsites.

About halfway along, observe a series of creeks flowing into Redwood Creek, including Bond Creek at about the 5.5-mile mark and Forty-Four Creek at 6.5 miles. The redwoods congregate in especially large families on the alluvial flats along Redwood Creek.

Nearly 8 miles along, the path crosses Redwood Creek on the last (summer-only) footbridge and meets Tall Trees Grove Trail. A left on this 1.1-mile long loop trail takes you to Howard Libbey, tallest in the grove.

Follow Redwood Creek through the heart of the park to Tall Trees Grove

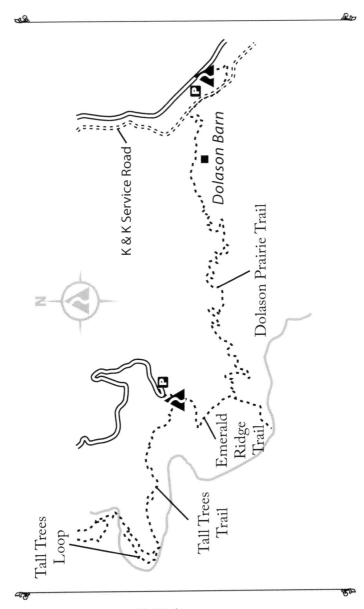

Tall Trees
Loop

Tall Trees
Trail

Emerald
Ridge
Trail

Dolason Prairie Trail

Dolason Barn

K & K Service Road

N

TheTrailmaster.com

TALL TREES GROVE
TALL TREES GROVE TRAIL

4.2 miles round trip with 500-foot elevation gain

A visit to the majestic colonnades of redwoods that form the heart of the national park is apt to be a humbling experience. Voices hush, children shush, eyes look skyward in reverence. It's little wonder that some hikers feel they've entered a natural cathedral and regard their time with the Tall Trees as a kind of spiritual experience.

After one of the 1960s' classic conservation battles, a narrow corridor of land along Redwood Creek was acquired to protect the world's highest trees. Taller trees were later discovered elsewhere in Redwood National and State Parks, but for decades Howard Libbey Tree (367.8 feet tall) in Tall Trees Grove was the tallest redwood accessible to the public.

While the 16.4-mile round trip adventure along Redwood Creek to the Tall Trees is a marvelous

all-day hike (or backpacking trip), Tall Trees Grove
Trail is a far easier way to go.

Easier to hike, that is. Getting to the trailhead is
a challenge—or part of the adventure as I see it.

A (free) permit is required to drive to the trailhead.
Obtain one of the limited number of permits from
Kuchel Visitor Center, the main park visitor center
near Orick. (Usually, even during the summer months,
sufficient permits are available for all who want to
make the drive and hike to the grove.) With the permit comes a combination (changed regularly) to a lock
on a gate across Tall Trees Grove Access Road.

DIRECTIONS: From the visitor center, travel
3 miles north on Highway 101 to Bald Hills Road.
Turn right and drive east 6.5 miles to Tall Trees
Grove Access Road and turn right. Use the combination given you to unlock the gate, close the gate behind you, and head 5.5 miles to the end of the gravel
road and parking.

A pavilion stands at road's end where there's a
sign-in book for hikers.

THE HIKE: From the parking area, the trail descends to reach a junction with Emerald Ridge Trail in
0.1 mile. Continue with Tall Trees Trail, which drops
rapidly and enters old-growth redwoods accompanied
by ferns and tangles of huckleberry. Showy (and large)
rhododendron color the dark forest.

The path hits bottom, so to speak, at a grouping of redwood giants. This collection and the handsome one near the junction of the Tall Trees Loop Trail and Redwood Creek Trail are among the standouts of Tall Trees Grove.

In summer, a footbridge spans Redwood Creek; walk across it and gain a great view of the tall trees from the far side of the creek.

Loop trail highlights include what was the tallest measured redwood. En route gaze at what were once considered the third-largest and sixth-largest *sempervirens*. After completing the loop, retrace your steps to the trailhead.

A fine example of the trailbuilders' handiwork: the bridge crossing over Forty Four Creek near a backcountry camp and Tall Trees Grove.

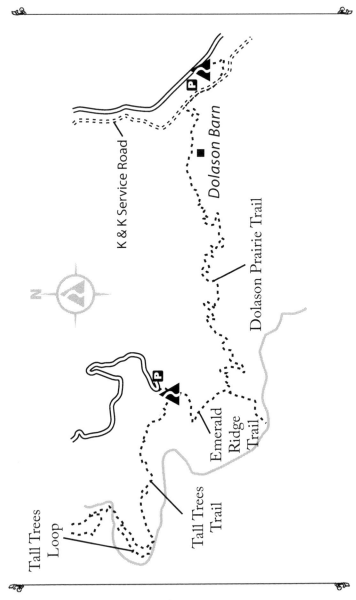

K & K Service Road

Dolason Barn

Dolason Prairie Trail

N

Emerald Ridge Trail

Tall Trees Trail

Tall Trees Loop

DOLASON PRAIRIE

DOLASON PRAIRIE TRAIL

To Lyons Barn is 2.2 miles round trip with 500-foot elevation gain; to Emerald Creek Bridge is 9 miles round trip with 1,900-foot gain

Captivating, little-traveled Dolason Prairie Trail descends from the Bald Hills to the redwoods and offers a tour of ancient redwoods, towering Douglas fir, oak woodland, wildflower-splashed meadows and a cascading creek. All this and an ocean view, too!

Once sheep pasture, Dolason Prairie is a spread of waist-high perennial grasses. As the story goes, 19th century rancher James Donaldson was the first to settle here; subsequent sheep ranchers slaughtered the spelling of his name. Still-standing Lyons Barn was constructed by sheep rancher Sherman Lyons in 1914 to shelter flocks during the rainy winters.

These days the prairie provides habitat for brush rabbits and the occasional Roosevelt elk.

This hike begins with crossing the prairie and grand views of Redwood Creek, descends to old-growth redwoods, and descends some more to meet Emerald Creek. From here you can head to Tall Trees Grove or descend Emerald Creek Trail to Redwood Creek.

This hike is downhill—a lot of downhill—first. The trail descends at nearly a 10 percent grade—a little less steep in the redwoods and a little more steep along the upper half of the path. That being said, the scenic wonders along this trail have been known to uplift weary legs and spirits and provide a psychic boost for the return trip.

DIRECTIONS: From Highway 101 in Orick, turn east on Bald Hills Road and drive 11 miles to the signed turnoff for Dolason Prairie Trail. Turn right into the parking lot and look for the path next to an information kiosk.

THE HIKE: The path immediately descends, leading over a Douglas fir-cloaked slope. At 0.5 mile, the path joins an old gravel logging road for 0.25 mile, then resumes as a footpath and continues through mixed woodland to Dolason Prairie and the picturesque Lyons Barn.

If it's clear down at the coast, the prairie's the place to partake of vistas of the canyon carved by Redwood Creek and the wide blue Pacific. Less inspiring is the view of clear-cut ridgetops (they're not called the Bald Hills for nothing), shorn of redwoods prior to the creation of Redwood National Park. As the path departs the prairie, oak-lovers will note the stand of Oregon white oak, which look a bit like smaller cousins of the valley oak.

For a mile or so, the path alternates between Douglas fir forest and grassland, then descends into dense forest where tanoak and madrone keep company with ancient redwoods and tall firs.

About 4.5 miles from the trailhead, the path crosses the sparkling waters of Emerald Creek on a wooden footbridge. Bordering the creek's dancing waters and quiet pools are dogwood and an assortment of ferns.

To extend the hike, cross Emerald Creek and ascend briefly to meet Emerald Ridge Trail. Go left 0.4 mile to Redwood Creek and right 0.9 miles to the trailhead for Tall Trees Trail. (See hike description.)

Once used as sheep pasture, Dolason Prairie now provides habitat for rabbits and Roosevelt elk.

Lady Bird
Johnson
Trail

Lady Bird
Johnson
Grove

N

Bald Hills Road

LADY BIRD JOHNSON GROVE

LADY BIRD JOHNSON GROVE LOOP TRAIL

**Loop around Lady Bird Johnson Grove is 1.3 miles
round trip**

Popular Lady Bird Johnson Loop Trail tours an
inspiring ridgetop redwood grove and offers a fine
introduction to the national park. Flat and easy, it's a
popular path because the trailhead is located close to
the main park visitor center and rangers frequently
recommend it to first-time visitors.

During her 1960s' stint as First Lady, Claudia
Taylor "Lady Bird" Johnson promoted many beauti-
fication and conservation projects, and was a staunch
advocate for the creation of Redwood National Park.
With her help, conservationists prevailed upon a re-
calcitrant Congress to acquire land for the new park.

In 1968, the First Lady attended the park dedication ceremony in what is now named Lady Bird
Johnson Grove. Somewhat ironically, it was her
husband Lyndon Johnson's successor and longtime

political foe President Richard Nixon who dedicated the grove to Lady Bird Johnson the following year.

But never mind politics. "Conservation is indeed a bipartisan business because all of us have the same stake in this magnificent continent," Johnson said at the dedication. "All of us have the same love for it and the same feeling that it is going to belong to our children and grandchildren and their grandchildren."

An easy, self-guiding nature trail loops through the redwoods that crown Bald Hills Ridge. Numerous benches en route offer a chance to rest and to contemplate the park below. Because of its elevation (1,200 feet) LBJ Grove is often fog-bound and enshrouded in mist—more so than lowland groves.

While hiking the trail (built for the park dedication ceremony) you emerge from the redwoods to gaze out past an ugly clear-cut to the coast. Much of the vista is now protected state and national park domain; it would no doubt all be Stump-Land had conservationists of the 1960s and after failed in their efforts.

FYI: There's another way to go to Lady Bird Johnson Grove. Berry Glen Trail (3 miles) ascends from Elk Prairie through old-growth and second-growth redwoods to the grove, meeting the nature trail near the park dedication site.

DIRECTIONS: From Kuchel Visitor Center, travel 3 miles north on Highway 101 to Bald Hills Road. Turn right and drive 2.7 miles on the steep narrow road and, after passing under a large foot-bridge, turn into the Lady Bird Johnson Grove parking area on the right side of the road.

THE HIKE: Begin by crossing Bald Hills Road on the handsome wooden pedestrian bridge. The path leads through a forest of redwood, Douglas fir and western hemlock.

About 0.2 mile out, the trail forks; bear left to begin a clockwise loop of the grove, treading past a lush undergrowth of sword ferns, salal, salmonberry, redwood sorrel and rhododendrons. At 0.6 mile the path reaches a clearing and park dedication site, as well as a signed junction with Berry Glen Trail.

Halfway along, the trail makes a hairpin turn and returns along the old-growth-forested north side of Bald Hills Ridge.

Makes you wonder why this hollow tree in LBJ Grove is still standing.

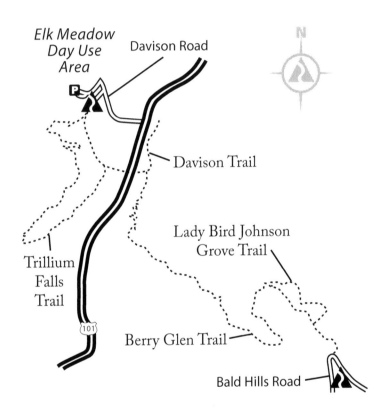

Elk Meadow
Day Use
Area

Davison Road

N

Davison Trail

Lady Bird Johnson
Grove Trail

Trillium
Falls
Trail

101

Berry Glen Trail

Bald Hills Road

BERRY GLEN

BERRY GLEN TRAIL

From Elk Meadow Day Use Area to Lady Bird Johnson Grove is 6 miles round trip with 1,200-foot elevation gain

Extending from Elk Meadow Day Use Area to Lady Bird Johnson Grove, Berry Glen Trail leads through old-growth and second-growth redwoods. "Berry Glen" was the locale of a 1930s-era family store known for its berry pies and a popular stop for Highway 101 travelers.

The upland redwoods are spaced just far enough apart so that sunlight (surprise!) plays upon the trees and trail. Numerous slants of light beam down upon the redwood slopes and the experience for the hiker, walking from light to dark and dark to light can be magical—particularly when fog or clouds diffuse the light.

Enjoy this hike as a moderate out-and-back from Elk Meadow to LBJ Grove or as an easy one-way (mostly downhill) hike from LBJ Grove to Elk Meadow. The latter route requires a car shuttle.

Hikers will be pleased to learn that not all funding from the American Recovery and Reinvestment Act went to building roads. At least a tiny portion of that stimulus funding went to building trails—among them Berry Glen Trail, completed in 2010.

Trail builders (California Conservation Corps) made good use of existing routes, including a portion of the original Bald Hills Road. It's a wide, smooth, built-to-government-spec trail. The relatively new path is a contrast to older redwood forest trails, which typically have lots of twists and turns, exposed roots and boggy places.

My only disappointment with the trail? No view. I guess with all that climbing and with relatively thin redwood groves I expected to get a panoramic view from the path.

DIRECTIONS: From Highway 101 in Orick, head 2.8 miles north to Davison Road. Turn west and drive 0.3 mile to plentiful parking at Elk Meadow Day Use Area. The signed trail begins at the south end of the large lot.

THE HIKE: Descend the paved hiking/biking path toward the meadow then bear right onto a paved road. In a short distance the road becomes dirt, leads alongside the meadow, then heads into the woods.

Cross Prairie Creek on a large wooden footbridge that also serves up great views of the Roosevelt elk. Sometimes the elk rest under the alder trees by the bridge.

Carefully cross Highway 101 and join signed Berry Glen Trail, which briefly follows the route of an old logging road then veers left and begins to ascend, soon leaving behind sight and sound of the highway.

The trail switchbacks through second-growth forest thick with huckleberry, climbs to an old-growth grove and ascends along a ridge. Eventually the path levels and travels into bigger trees, accompanied by patches of tall ferns.

Following the route of an old road, the path passes numerous big trees and junctions Lady Bird Johnson Grove Nature Trail very close to the grove's dedication plaque. Loop around the nature trail to the LBJ parking area and/or return the way you came.

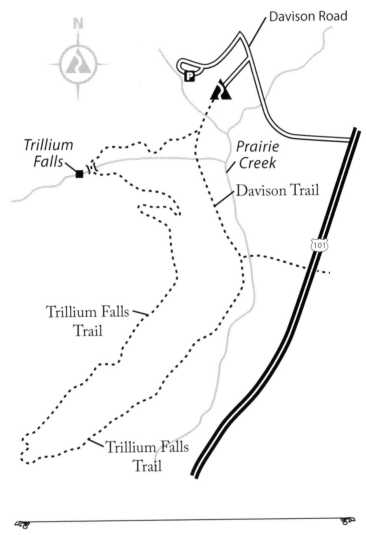

Davison Road

N

Trillium
Falls

Prairie
Creek

Davison Trail

101

Trillium Falls
Trail

Trillium Falls
Trail

TRILLIUM FALLS

TRILLIUM FALLS TRAIL

From Elk Meadow Day Use Area, a 2.5-mile loop with 300-foot elevation gain

One of the park's more popular pathways, well-built Trillium Falls Trail loops through impressive groves of old-growth redwoods. Additional attractions include elk-viewing opportunities and Trillium Falls, a modest 10-foot cascade that spills over moss-covered boulders.

Western trillium is one of the North Coast's iconic wildflowers and it's quite a sight when it blooms in the spring—particularly along the creek. Aptly named, it's tri- (three)-leaved with large pointed leaves and has three petals that are bright white in first bloom then shade to pink and purplish hues.

Considering that the trailhead for this hike was once the site of an Arcata Redwood Company sawmill, it's a pleasant surprise indeed to discover so many big trees still standing. And the redwoods do not stand alone. Handsome big-leaf maples, Douglas-fir, western hemlock, and Sitka spruce reside near and sometimes under the shade of the redwoods.

Two downsides to this hike: more traffic noise than you'd expect hiking a redwood sanctuary and don't hold your breath looking for Roosevelt elk. The animals seem to prefer to graze elsewhere and the large parking lot for potential elk-viewers is often empty.

DIRECTIONS: From Highway 101 in Orick, head 2.8 miles north to Davison Road. Turn west and drive 0.3 mile to plentiful parking at Elk Meadow Day Use Area. The signed trail begins at the south end of the large lot.

THE HIKE: From the southern end of the parking lot, walk one of the paved pathways to meet Davison Trail, bear right and, in a hundred yards, reach signed Trillium Falls Trail.

Begin a mild ascent with switchbacks into redwood forest with congregations of quite large trees. About 0.6 mile from the trailhead, cross a long steel bridge and behold Trillium Falls tumbling down a rocky, maple-lined ravine.

Another modest climb leads 0.6 mile to John B. DeWitt Grove, named for the longtime secretary of the Save-the-Redwoods League.

From the grove, the trail drops 0.2 mile to cross a gravel road and continues descending through impressive redwoods (the biggest trees thrive at the south end of the loop trail) and also amidst mixed woodland of red alder, hazel, and big leaf maple.

The trail turns north and, at the 2.5-mile mark, the trail meets that dirt road again and it's adios to the redwoods. Travel 0.3 mile on the alder-lined road to complete your journey.

For a short and scenic detour, turn right on the trail to Prairie Creek Bridge. From the viewing platform built into the bridge, enjoy vistas of the creek and scout the terrain for Roosevelt Elk. (BTW Berry Glen Trail heads this way, crosses the highway and ascends redwood-filled slopes to Lady Bird Johnson Grove. See hike description.) Retrace your steps to meet the road and follow it back to the trailhead.

Trillium Falls Trail: the journey is even better than the destination!

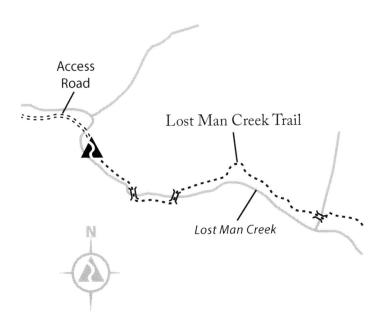

Access
Road

Lost Man Creek Trail

Lost Man Creek

N

LOST MAN CREEK

Along Lost Man Creek is 2 miles round trip.

A lovely tumbling creek, rocky pools and a lush forest are highlights of Lost Man Creek, one of the park's less discovered gems. Keep company with impressive redwoods along this creekside trail named for a timber locator who never returned.

DIRECTIONS: From Highway 101, 4 miles north of Orick, turn east and follow a gravel road 2 miles to Lost Man Creek Picnic Area.

THE HIKE: Slip past a hiker stile, pass the picnic ground, and begin a gentle climb through the forest. A quarter-mile out, the path crosses an old bridge over Lost Man Creek. Admire the view up-creek of the handsome watercourse.

Ascend through a mixed forest of redwoods and Douglas fir until the road begins to climb uphill toward a logged area. This is trail's end for the pretty part of the path and the usual turnaround point.

*Prairie Creek Redwoods SP is crisscrossed
by fern-lined footpaths.*

EVERY TRAIL TELLS A STORY.

II
PRAIRIE CREEK
REDWOODS STATE PARK

HIKE ON.

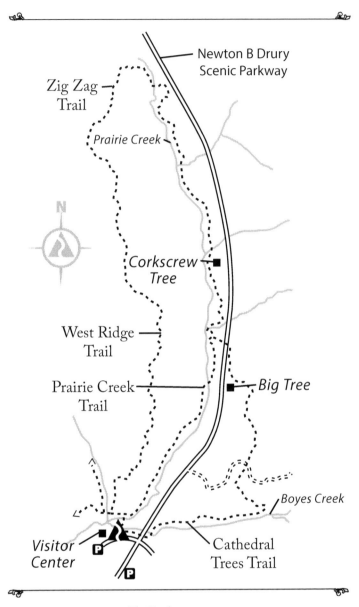

Newton B Drury
Scenic Parkway

Zig Zag
Trail

Prairie Creek

N

*Corkscrew
Tree*

West Ridge
Trail

Prairie Creek
Trail

Big Tree

Boyes Creek

*Visitor
Center*

P

P

Cathedral
Trees Trail

TheTrailmaster.com

CATHEDRAL TREES

CATHEDRAL TREES, FOOTHILL TRAILS

2.7-mile loop with 200-foot elevation gain

Call it Big Tree Loop, Cathedral Trees Loop, or Stop 'n Gawk. By whatever name, this loop offers the time-short or leg-weary visitor an ideal way to experience mighty large trees on a relatively short hike.

This hike packs-in the highlights and may be the best sampling of tall trees in the parks—Redwood National Park in general, Prairie Creek Redwoods State Park in particular. Kids like this hike because of its jungle-like environs—ferns, moss-draped maples and, of course, the cathedrals.

Ah, the Cathedral Trees, those splendid congregations of redwoods. No wonder John Muir (who named Cathedral Peak and Cathedral Lake in Yosemite) and other naturalists were always using religious imagery to describe natural features. Cathedral trees are groups of trees that have grown up from the living remains of the stump of a fallen redwood;

because they grew from the perimeter of a round stump, they are arranged in a circle.

You can jump right on Cathedral Trees Trail (1.4 miles) at the Big Tree Wayside parking area but it's better to ease into the trees by starting the hike from Prairie Creek Visitor Center.

The loop includes Circle Trail (0.3 mile) definitely the best and easiest 15-minute tour of the redwoods: a lush redwood forest and easy access to the Big Tree, one of the largest redwoods in Prairie Creek Redwoods State Park. A 100-yard long walkway leads to Big Tree, which stands 304 feet tall and measures 21 feet in diameter.

Frankly, while I love Cathedral Trees Trail, I never hike the same loop twice. So feel free to improvise: for example, if you're one of those hikers who can't get enough of Prairie Creek Trail, consider trekking that terrific trail coming or going in combination with Cathedral Trees Trail.

DIRECTIONS: From Highway 101 about 4 miles north of Orick, exit onto the Newton B. Drury Scenic Parkway. Drive 0.5 mile to the signed entrance for Prairie Creek State Park. Turn west and drive 0.1 mile to the campground entry/kiosk and to the Elk Prairie Visitor Center. Park in one of the two lots on either side of the road.

THE HIKE: From the trailhead next to the park entry road, hike east on the combined Cathedral Trees Trail/Elk Prairie Loop. The trail dips under the parkway through a tunnel and crosses Boyes Creek.

At 0.2 mile, bear right on signed Foothill Trail. Stick with Cathedral Trees Trail at another junction at 0.4 mile and continue to the many family groupings known as cathedrals. Meander through this sanctuary of trees, which also includes fallen trees that have become nursery logs for a wide variety of trees and ferns.

Cross Cal Barrel Road at 1.1 mile and meet Circle Trail at 1.5 mile out. Check out Big Tree and head out on Foothill Trail, a fairly flat former wagon road, re-cross Cal Barrel Road and visit Rotary Grove.

Continue through the forest, close the loop, and return to the trailhead via the combined Cathedral Trees Trail/Elk Prairie Loop.

James Irvine Trail

Clintonia Trail

Miners' Ridge Trail

Newton B Drury Parkway

TheTrailmaster.com

MINER'S RIDGE

JAMES IRVINE, CLINTONIA, MINER'S RIDGE TRAILS

7.3 miles round trip loop with 400-foot elevation gain

Hike a trio of trails to redwoods high on a ridge and down in a lush canyon bottom on this grand tour of Prairie Creek Redwoods State Park.

Begin on James Irvine Trail, which leads into the redwood forest primeval. A number of bridges help keep your boots dry at creek crossings and add to the aesthetics of this handsomely designed trail. Back in the mid-19th century this route had a more utilitarian function: the path was used by miners to get to (not-very lucrative) claims at Gold Bluffs Beach.

BTW, the full length of James Irvine Trail (4.5 miles) makes an excellent and easy one-way hike from the Prairie Creek Redwoods State Park visitor center to the beach at Fern Canyon. It's a Trailmaster favorite. And if you're pressed for time, even a short out-and-back on the trail is worthwhile.

Clintonia Trail, named for the fuchsia in the vicinity, connects the James Irvine and Miner's Ridge trails. From Miner's Ridge, hikers gain grand vistas of redwood forests, the coast, and the wide blue Pacific.

DIRECTIONS: From Highway 101 about 4 miles north of Orick, exit onto the Newton B. Drury Scenic Parkway. Drive 0.5 mile to the signed entrance for Prairie Creek State Park. Turn west and drive 0.1 mile to the campground entry/kiosk and to the Elk Prairie Visitor Center. Park in one of the two lots on either side of the road and walk past the visitor center to the main trailhead.

THE HIKE: From the Visitor Center, take the Nature Trail and soon cross Prairie Creek on a high wooden footbridge. Pass right-branching Prairie Creek Trail in 0.1 mile, a junction with West Ridge Trail at 0.2 mile, and cross Godwood Creek to soon reach signed James Irvine Trail.

The path rises, dips to cross a tributary of Godwood Creek on a footbridge, then rises again, switchbacking across the west side of Miner's Ridge and reaching a junction with left-forking Miner's Ridge Trail (this hike's return route.)

Hike among the ancient redwoods, enjoy vistas of old-growth forest en route—particularly down-slope along Godwood Creek and watch for other arboreal companions: Douglas fir, western hemlock, tanoak and maple.

At the 2.2 mile mark, reach Yamas Grove and an inviting bench. Duck under a redwood fallen across the trail as you pass through an area of blow-downs, travel the canyon bottom a mile, descend steps and cross a creek to reach the signed junction with Clintonia Trail.

Ascend Clintonia Trail 0.5 mile though a lovely and more open redwood forest to crest Miner's Ridge. The path travels another 0.7 mile through partially logged (gasp) forest to meet Miner's Ridge Trail. Turn left, soon regain the ridgeline, and enjoy wonderful vistas of slopes thick with redwoods.

The trail descends a final 0.5 or so to meet James Irvine Trail. From here retrace your steps a mile back to the trailhead.

If there was a vote for "Best Park Trail," James Irvine Trail would win a lot of votes!

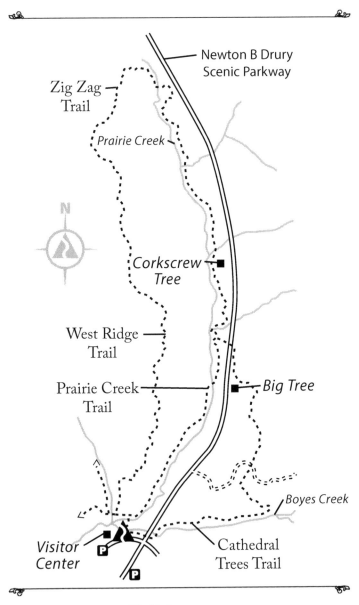

Newton B Drury
Scenic Parkway

Zig Zag
Trail

Prairie Creek

N

*Corkscrew
Tree*

West Ridge
Trail

Prairie Creek
Trail

Big Tree

Boyes Creek

Visitor
Center

Cathedral
Trees Trail

WEST RIDGE & PRAIRIE CREEK

WEST RIDGE, ZIG ZAG #1, AND PRAIRIE CREEK TRAILS

5.8 mile loop with 600 foot elevation gain

This hike delivers grand scenery thanks to West Ridge Trail and Prairie Creek Trail, two of the premiere paths in Prairie Creek Redwoods State Park. Connecting the two is a series of tight switchbacks known as Zig Zag # 1 Trail.

West Ridge Trail weaves across a redwood-cloaked, fern-filled ridge. You'll hike an intriguing length of this 7-mile long trail that leads through awe-inspiring old-growth redwoods.

Prairie Creek Trail alternates between dense redwood groves and open riverbank flora, crossing Prairie Creek numerous times. The banks are shaded with maple trees, bright green in summer, mellow yellow in autumn, and in all seasons a lovely counterpoint to the dark and solemn redwoods.

This hike has a lot of variety with airy ridges and longish (for the redwoods anyway) vistas, as well as the broad canyon of Prairie Creek and cathedral groves with very tall trees. A number of handy—and handsome—footbridges offer safe passage over creeks and places to contemplate the inspirational scene. Plus memorable trees, including Corkscrew Tree with its medley of twisted trunks.

DIRECTIONS: From Highway 101 about 4 miles north of Orick, exit onto the Newton B. Drury Scenic Parkway. Drive 0.5 mile to the signed entrance for Prairie Creek State Park. Turn west and drive 0.1 mile to the campground entry/kiosk and to the Elk Prairie Visitor Center. Park in one of the two lots.

THE HIKE: From the signed trailhead behind the visitor center, cross the bridge over Prairie Creek and junction Prairie Creek Trail (your return route) on the right in 0.1 mile. Stay left and soon join signed West Ridge Trail.

After brief passage on the forest floor, the trail begins an aggressive switchbacking ascent of West Ridge, gaining the ridgeline about a mile from the trailhead. The path stays on or near the ridge top, serving up impressive redwood forest vistas over both sides of the ridge.

At the 2.4-mile mark, meet Zig Zag Trail #1 on the right. (Before joining this connector trail continue another 200 feet or so to reach a bench with a plaque that simply reads: "Forever." Trailside views take in aptly named Godwood Creek, and a canyon full of huge stately trees.

Descend 0.5 mile on Zig Zag Trail #1. About halfway down the switchbacks, hike among impressive trees and enjoy the vistas of the Prairie Creek valley floor.

Turn right on signed Prairie Creek Trail. The down-creek route passes large redwoods the Tunnel Log, and a junction at Brown Creek with a side trail leading to Newton Drury Parkway (traffic noise can diminish the tranquility of the trail along Prairie Creek).

Step off the trail to view the Corkscrew Tree, and continue another 1.6 miles along Prairie Creek to close the loop and return to the visitor center.

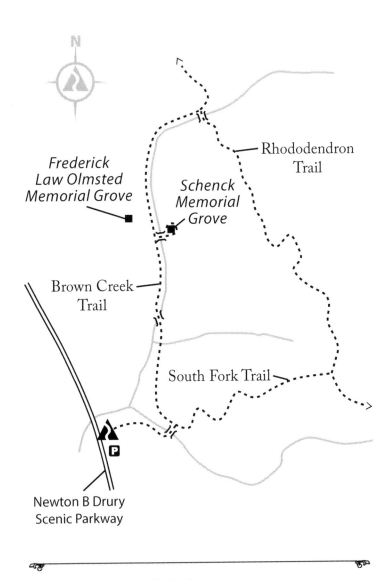

N

Rhododendron
Trail

Frederick
Law Olmsted
Memorial Grove

Schenck
Memorial
Grove

Brown Creek
Trail

South Fork Trail

Newton B Drury
Scenic Parkway

BROWN CREEK

SOUTH FORK, RHODODENDRON, BROWN CREEK TRAILS

3.5-mile loop with 500-foot elevation gain

Brown Creek, a tributary of far-better-known Prairie Creek, flows past stands of mighty redwoods. In the right light (a sunny day), the redwoods and the green creekside flora combine to create a magical forest.

By magical I mean both the ancient trees and accompanying profusion of flora—ferns, mushrooms, moss and redwood sorrel—that spring from enormous "nursery" logs. Oh, those towering redwoods! You can't quite see the tops of the tall trees and often you can't quite see end to end along one of the fallen giants, engulfed as they are by the ultra-lush understory.

Near Brown Creek are two memorial groves of big redwoods named for big-time conservationists: Trees of the Great Grove, dedicated to Carl Alwyn Schenck (1868-1955), founder of the first forestry school in the US, and a grove honoring Frederick Olmstead, famed landscape architect, designer of Central Park and a co-founder of the Save-the-Redwoods League.

A trio of trails forms an engaging loop. Short but scenic South Fork Trail ascends into the redwoods. Rhododendron Trail features the bright pink and red blooms (mid spring to early summer) of the rhododendron en route. The flowers are all the more lovely in the midst of the dark redwoods and the lush green flora beneath them. And Brown Creek Trail delivers the hiker to big trees and burbling Brown Creek.

And what's not to like about this loop? It's easily accessible yet removed from the hum of Highway 101 traffic. It's long enough to "really see something" yet short enough to hike even if you're pressed for time. It's definitely low traffic compared to other short hikes; perhaps the stiff ascent up South Fork Trail discourages casual tourists.

DIRECTIONS: From Highway 101, about 5 miles north of Orick, exit on Newton B. Drury Parkway. Drive 2.7 miles to a pullout (right after the Big Trees pullout) and the signed trailhead for South Fork Trail.

THE HIKE: South Fork Trail ascends 0.2 mile before passing a junction with Brown Creek Trail (your return route) and the left. Short and steep and sweet South Fork Trail ends in a mile at a junction with Rhododendron Trail. Turn left here and join Rhododendron Trail, which dips into and out of a redwood-filled ravine, and passes amidst more tall trees on a descent to Brown Creek. The redwoods thriving near the creek are particularly impressive.

Follow Rhododendron Trail over a footbridge spanning Brown Creek and junction Brown Creek Trail. Turn left and begin a mellow descent along the creek. The trees appear to get larger and larger with the descent. About a half-mile down the trail note a side trail on the left crossing Brown Creek; it leads to a memorial grove.

Continue on the main path as it crosses Brown Creek and curves to meet South Fork Trail, which you follow 0.2 mile back to the trailhead.

Ferns, rhododendrons, soothing waters—a tranquil trail indeed.

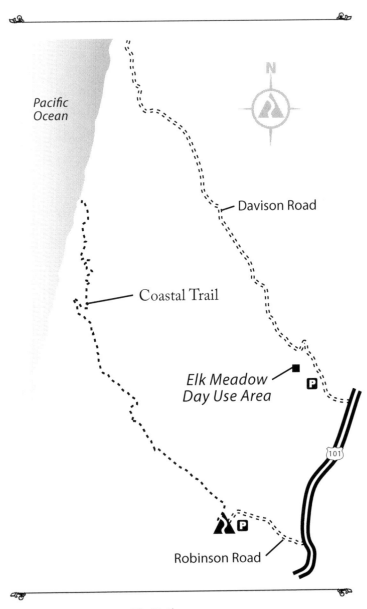

Pacific
Ocean

N

Davison Road

Coastal Trail

Elk Meadow
Day Use Area

P

101

Robinson Road

P

SKUNK CABBAGE CREEK
SKUNK CABBAGE (COASTAL) TRAIL

To Gold Bluff Beach is 7.8 miles round trip with 600-foot elevation gain; to Davison Road is 10.5 miles round trip

Moss-draped Sitka spruce and a multitude of skunk cabbage massed on the muddy flats by Skunk Cabbage Creek make this a rainforest-like ramble to remember. After Skunk Cabbage Trail tours this lush jungle, it delivers a second delight: Gold Bluffs Beach, where miles of dark, driftwood-strewn sand offer a second coastal adventure.

Many hikers would opine that the Skunk Cabbage section is the most enchanting length of Coastal Trail in Redwood National and State Parks. It feels wonderfully remote. Among the surprises in the luxuriant forest are Roosevelt elk, more commonly sighted in the prairies along Highway 101.

The skunk cabbage appears to be a pituitary freak of the plant world: some specimens measure more than four feet across, with foot-long leaves. In the tall tree-filtered light, the cabbages glow an otherworldly green. Turns out, the skunk cabbage is not a science experiment gone awry, but a botanic cousin to the corn lily. Some skunk cabbages grow along their namesake trail; many more crowd the banks of their namesake creek.

Some hikers like to arrange a ride back and walk up-coast to meet Davison Road, where it descends to Gold Bluffs Beach. With a car shuttle, this offers one-way hiking possibilities.

DIRECTIONS: From Highway 101, about 2 miles north of Orick (and just north of the turnoff on the right for Bald Hills Road), turn left (west) on the signed park road for Skunk Cabbage/Coastal Trail and drive 0.75 to the dirt road's end at the parking area and trailhead.

THE HIKE: The alder-lined, mostly level trail probes a very green world. About 0.5-mile out, where the path closely parallels the creek, look for masses of skunk cabbages, sprouting head to head from the boggy ground.

The trail repeatedly crosses and re-crosses Skunk Cabbage Creek, traveling amongst Sitka spruce and occasional old redwoods that escaped the loggers. Ferns floor the forest primeval.

After two miles, the trail suddenly climbs out of a narrow, fern-filled canyon and up a forested ridge. Even more suddenly, the forest fades, you reach a trail junction at 2.4 miles, and there's Gold Bluffs Beach at your feet. Well, almost at your feet. While a sketchy trail does switchback 0.25-mile down the bluffs to the beach, it's long been officially closed to travel.

The main Skunk Cabbage Trail climbs a bit more before descending and then dipping in and out of two fern-filled canyons. Finally the path emerges from the lush vegetation to meet Gold Bluffs Beach. A substantial sign is posted here (so beach hikers can find Skunk Cabbage Trail).

The intrepid hiker can walk north many more miles along the wild and windswept beach. If you've arranged for a pickup, trek about 1.5 miles up-coast and then over the dunes to meet Davison Road.

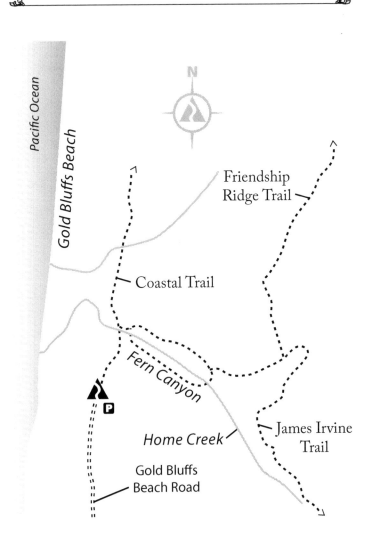

Pacific Ocean

Gold Bluffs Beach

N

Friendship
Ridge Trail

Coastal Trail

Fern Canyon

Home Creek

James Irvine
Trail

Gold Bluffs
Beach Road

FERN CANYON

FERN CANYON LOOP TRAIL

Loop through Fern Canyon is 1 mile round trip

Of the several beautiful "fern canyons" found along the North Coast, Fern Canyon in Prairie Creek Redwoods State Park is undoubtedly the most awe-inspiring. Five-finger, deer, lady, sword, and chain ferns smother the precipitous walls of the canyon. Bright yellow monkey-flowers abound, as well as fairy lanterns, those creamy white, or greenish, bell-shaped flowers that hang in clusters.

Ferns are descendants of an ancient group of plants that were more numerous 200 million years ago. Ferns have roots and stems similar to flowering plants, but are considered to be a primitive form of plant life because they reproduce by spores, not seeds.

Lovely as it is, the size and shape of Fern Canyon did not occur naturally. Hydraulic miners of the late 19th century turned high- pressure cannons on the canyon walls, washing away the soil in order to uncover gold. Getting hosed left the canyon with a level bottom and narrow, near-perpendicular walls.

Fortunately nature rebounded big-time from this hydro-assault and today there's hardly a centimeter of canyon wall not smothered in greenery—particularly ferns.

The trail is of lollipop loop configuration. Hike the whole loop or go to the top of Fern Canyon and return the way you came to repeat the most intriguing segment of the trail.

Expect company, lots of it, in the summer when the wooden footbridges are up and everybody and their brother from Iowa and sister from Italy does this hike. Come back in the off-season when the bridges are down if you want solitude in Fern Canyon.

DIRECTIONS: From Highway 101, 3 miles north of Orick, turn west on Davison Road. The dirt, washboard road descends logged slopes and through second-growth redwoods 4 miles to the Gold Bluffs Beach and park entry station (day use fee). Drive 4 more miles to the end of the road at a parking lot (which can fill up at the height of the summer travel season) for Fern Canyon Trailhead. Restrooms are here, as well access to the beach.

THE HIKE: The path leads along the pebbled floor of Fern Canyon. In the wettest places, the route follows wooden planks across Home Creek. With sword and five-finger ferns pointing the way, you pass through marshy areas covered with wetlands grass and dotted with a bit of skunk cabbage. Lurking about are Pacific giant salamanders.

A half-mile from the trailhead, the path climbs out of the canyon on wooden steps to intersect James Irvine Trail. A mile or two out and back amidst dense redwood forest is a great addition to Fern Canyon Trail. James Irvine Trail (see hike description) crosses to the south side of the canyon proceeds southeast with Home Creek. The trail reaches the upper neck of Fern Canyon, and continues to its upper trailhead near the park visitor center.

To continue with the loop, travel 0.25 mile through the forest and loop back around to the mouth of Fern Canyon.

Fern Canyon: A hanging garden of ferns graces the forest primeval.

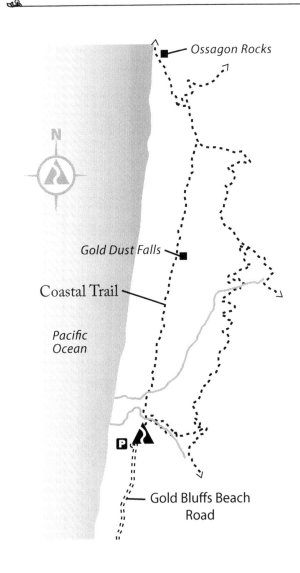

Ossagon Rocks

Gold Dust Falls

Coastal Trail

Pacific
Ocean

Gold Bluffs Beach
Road

GOLD BLUFFS BEACH

COASTAL TRAIL

From Fern Canyon to Gold Dust Falls is 2 miles round trip; to Butler Creek is 4.5 miles round trip; to Ossagon Rocks is 6 miles round trip

Wildlife-watching, waterfalls and a wilderness beach are just a few of the highlights of a hike along the northern reaches of Gold Bluffs Beach. While even one of these en route attractions makes for a compelling hike, the mere prospect of so many engaging environments can put a hiker into sensory overload before reaching the trailhead.

Gold Bluffs Beach (both bluffs and beach) is prime Roosevelt elk territory. While nearby elk-viewing opportunities abound, the creatures seem all the more majestic in this wilderness setting.

Waterfalls near the coast are a rarity, so the presence of three of them in close proximity to Coastal Trail is a special treat indeed. Gold Dust Falls, a long, slender tumbler, spills some 80 feet to the forest floor.

An unnamed waterfall is located just south of Gold Dust; another is located just north.

In the case of this hike, the journey overshadows the destination; nevertheless, the destination—the odd Ossagon Rocks—are intriguing in their own way. The rocks resemble sea stacks, though they're positioned right at land's end, not in their usual offshore location.

DIRECTIONS: From Highway 101 in Orick, drive 2 miles north to signed Davison Road. Turn left (west) and proceed 7 miles to road's end at the Prairie Creek Redwoods State Park Fern Canyon trailhead.

THE HIKE: Coastal Trail begins on the other side of Home Creek, an easy ford in summer, but may present a challenge during the rainy season. Usually a signpost on the north side of the creek shows the way to the start of Coastal Trail.

Join the path for a brief meander through the forest then out across the grass-topped dunes. The hiker is often out of sight of the surf, but never altogether removed from its thunderous roll, even when the Coastal Trail strays 0.1 mile inland.

A mile out, the sound of falling water and an unsigned path forking right into the forest calls you to Coastal Trail's first cascade, a long, wispy waterfall framed by ferns.

Another 0.25 mile along the main path leads to the short connector trail leading to Gold Dust Falls.

A well-placed bench offers repose and a place to contemplate the inspiring cataract. A minute or so more down the main trail delivers you to another brief spur trail and the third of Coastal Trail's cascades.

Coastal Trail edges from prairie to forest and reaches Butler Creek and a retired campsite at 2.25 miles. This pleasant spot is located at a convergence of environments—creekside alder woodland, a prairie matted with head-high native grasses, the creek mouth and the beach beyond.

Cross Butler Creek and travel the grassy sand verbena-topped prairie for a final 0.5 mile to cross Ossagon Creek and junction with Ossagon Trail. Continue on Coastal Trail a bit farther north, then bid adieu to the path and head oceanward to Ossagon Rocks.

What a beach to hike! A black sand strand backed by golden bluffs.

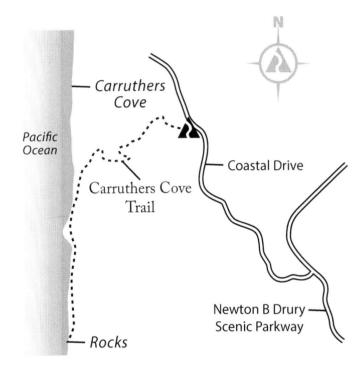

Pacific
Ocean

N

— Carruthers
Cove

Carruthers Cove
Trail

— Coastal Drive

— Rocks

Newton B Drury —
Scenic Parkway

COASTAL TRAIL

CARRUTHERS COVE TRAIL

From Coastal Drive to Carruthers Cove is 1.6 miles round trip with 500-foot elevation gain

"Bad roads. Good hike."

That could be one way to provide a capsule description of the road to the trailhead and the trail to Carruthers Cove.

Coastal Drive (once upon a time, Highway 101) is the route to the trailhead. It was bypassed because of its propensity to slide into the Pacific. Even today, the road looks like it needs a bit of repair—potholes, wide cracks, buckled pavement. In my view, such imperfections just add to the sense of adventure, and I hope the road is kept in a kind of arrested decay, just safe enough for travel.

The other "bad" road is the logging skid road that extends from Coastal Drive to Carruthers Cove. The hike to Carruthers Cove begins as a footpath and ends as a footpath; the middle is reworked skid road.

Carruthers: In the land of the redwoods, where so many features are named for timber barons or outside-the-area industrialists and philanthropists, it's refreshing to find a feature named for a local, newspaperman J.H. Crothers.

Distinguished newspaper publisher J.H. Crothers, a significant business leader in Humboldt County during the first half of the 20th century, owned the cliffside property above misnamed Carruthers Cove.

On a foggy June day in 1916 the steamship *Bear* en route from Portland to San Francisco ran aground near Cape Mendocino. The vessel's cargo included hundreds of tons of newsprint. John Holyoke Crothers, owner of The Humboldt Times, purchased it for $500 and hired local ranchers to pull the thousand-pound paper rolls from the surf and haul them up to Eureka, where he used the paper to print his newspaper and start the Humboldt Paper Company.

Once you hit the beach, you can walk north about a half mile north before the cliffs block further passage. Better beach-hiking is available to the south; a 2-mile walk (at low tide only) leads to Ossagon Rocks (see hike description).

DIRECTIONS: From Highway 101, 5 miles north of Orick, exit on Newton B. Drury Parkway and drive about 8 miles north to Coastal Drive. Turn left (west) and travel 1 mile to a turnout and signed trailhead on the left.

THE HIKE: Descend on the trail, once the old logging road, and pass among second-growth redwoods, as well as alder and Sitka spruce. The trees obscure vistas of the coast. You might smell the salt-tanged ocean air before you actually see the ocean.

After a mellow start, the descent steepens. Near the beach, the scenery transitions from upland forest to grasses, coastal shrubs and a sprinkling of sea rockets.

Then voila! Behold the sand strand of Carruthers Cove, bold sea stacks thrusting up from the Pacific surf, and a wetland located at the mouth of Johnson Creek and bounded by a sea stack.

At Carruthers Cove, dramatic meeting of land and sea.

At the mouth of Damnation Creek, find a dramatic coastline a whole lot of cow parsnip.

EVERY TRAIL TELLS A STORY.

III
NORTHERN
REDWOODS NP

HIKE ON.

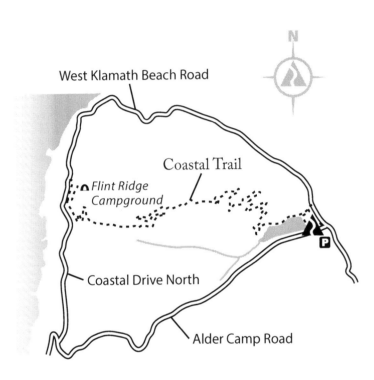

West Klamath Beach Road

N

Coastal Trail

⌂ *Flint Ridge
Campground*

Coastal Drive North

Alder Camp Road

P

Flint Ridge

Coastal Trail

From Douglas Memorial Bridge site to Flint Ridge Campground is 9 miles round trip with 800-foot elevation gain

Historians note that in pre-park days the magnificent redwoods on Flint Ridge were considered as the centerpiece for a Redwood National Park. Alas, timber companies toppled many of the big trees before the national park got off the drawing board.

That being said, plenty of trees remain to be seen along this hike through the redwoods and across a ridge to the mouth of the Klamath River. The path, once known as Flint Ridge Trail is now officially the Flint Ridge Section of the Coastal Trail.

At the trailhead, pause for homage to Douglas Memorial Bridge that once spanned the Klamath River. Constructed in 1926, the handsome arch bridge served Highway 101 travelers until destroyed by the great flood of 1964.

The trail begins near Marshall Pond, a onetime millpond, now known to have pretty good bird-watching. Ducks patrol the pond, fringed by thickets of blackberries.

Flint Ridge Camp, located at the west end of the trail, boasts 11 sites, picnic tables and toilets. (No water, though; keep that in mind, campers and hikers.) The camp is an easy walk-in (less than 0.25 mile) from Coastal Drive.

DIRECTIONS: From Highway 101, just south of those long bridges spanning the Klamath River, head west 1.6 miles on Klamath Beach Road to a junction with Alder Camp Road. Look for a small lot and the trailhead across from the Douglas Memorial Bridge site.

THE HIKE: Head northeast into a thick woodland of red alder. Watch for a beaver dam as the path approaches Marshall Pond. The trail meets a dirt road and after two left turns traces the north shore of the pond.

Resuming as a footpath it ascends to redwoods at the first switchback, and more and more redwoods with the switchbacks that follow on the climb up Flint Ridge. At your feet is redwood sorrel and salal, while high above your head soar mighty redwoods (some measuring 12-feet in diameter) as well as some by-no-means-diminutive Douglas fir.

Around the 2-mile mark, the path gains the ridgeline and offers a vista of the impressive canyon of the Klamath River. The trail sticks close to, and just south of, the ridgetop. As the path descends, pass more large redwoods, a mixture of environs including second-growth redwoods, a slice of logged-over forest and then finally a lush forest scene highlighted by red alder in company with ferns and spruce.

Near the end of the hike, you'll hear the roar of Pacific breakers. A short spur trail leads to Flint Ridge Camp. A bit beyond the camp, the trail ends at Coastal Drive across from a small parking lot.

Flint Ridge Camp beckons backpackers and day hikers along the Redwood Coastal Trail.

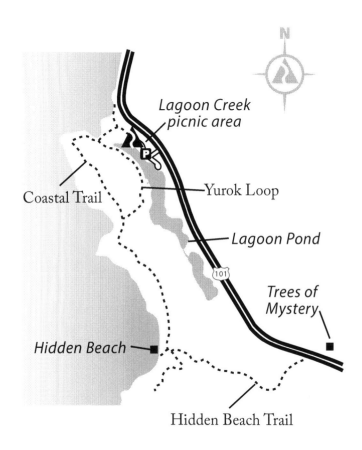

Lagoon Creek
picnic area

Yurok Loop

Coastal Trail

Lagoon Pond

101

Trees of
Mystery

Hidden Beach

Hidden Beach Trail

N

Hidden Beach and Requa Overlook

Coastal Trail

From Lagoon Creek to Hidden Beach is 2 miles round trip; to Requa Overlook is 7.8 miles round trip with 500-foot gain

One of the more spectacular sections of Coastal Trail in RNSP is the 4-mile length between Lagoon Creek and the mouth of the Klamath River. The "Hidden Beach Section" of the Coastal Trail extends along high, steep, spruce-spiked cliffs rising far above the breakers.

The trail tunnels through a dense tangle of ferns and blackberry bushes, emerging to offer ocean views. Inhale the salty air, hear the sea lions bark, and savor the splendid coastal scene.

For a short hike, head for Hidden Beach, a peaceful little cove with a sandy beach. For a longer hike, follow Coastal Trail to a picnic area and a stunning view of the mouth of the Klamath River from Requa Overlook.

Trailhead for this jaunt is Lagoon Creek, which empties into a pond formed in 1940 when a lumber mill dammed the creek. Heart-shaped yellow pond lilies float in the tranquil pond, habitat for ducks, egrets, herons and red-winged blackbirds.

Long ago the pond was a lake—O-kwego, as it was known by the Yurok, who lived in a village located near what is now the Yurok Loop trailhead. Although many aspects of their tribal life traditionally centered on the banks of the Klamath River, the Yurok also had several settlements along the coast.

Yurok Loop Trail explores the lagoon area. For variety, use the coastal half of the loop on departure and the inland half on return.

DIRECTIONS: Lagoon Creek Fishing Access is located west of Highway 101, 6.9 miles north of the Klamath River Bridge, and just north of the Trees of Mystery.

THE HIKE: From the picnic area, hike across a footbridge at the edge of the lagoon. The path soon splits. The left-fork of the trail leads along the edge of lagoon and is pretty enough but the din of traffic from Highway 101 is an assault on the senses.

Take the right fork and travel south. From breaks in the bluff-top vegetation, get great views of sea stacks and the rocky shoreline below.

Coastal Trail veers right from Yurok Trail and follows a fern-lined path to a grove of red alder. During spring and summer, hikers may observe hummingbirds extracting nectar from pink-flowered salmonberry bushes.

A mile from the trailhead, reach the turn-off to Hidden Beach, a driftwood-piled sandy beach that's ideal for a picnic. Hike on, pass a left forking path (Hidden Beach Trail) that leads to Trees of Mystery, and ascend into Sitka spruce forest.

Halfway to Requa Overlook, Coastal Trail crests a divide and continues on through thick forest and lots of blackberry bushes. Occasional overlooks offer glimpses of the bold headlands north and south, wave-cut terraces, sea lions and seals hauled-out on offshore rocks.

Coastal Trail angles southeast to Requa Overlook, offering picnic sites and impressive views of the mouth of the Klamath River.

From Yurok Loop Trail, get great coastal views.

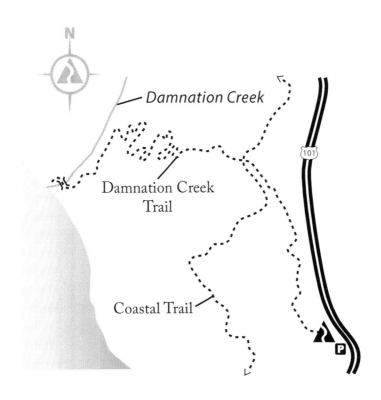

Damnation Creek

Damnation Creek Trail

Coastal Trail

101

Damnation Creek

Damnation Creek Trail

From Highway 101 to Damnation Cove is 4.5 miles round trip with 1,000-foot elevation gain

In the Damnation Creek watershed, Del Norte Coast Redwoods State Park delivers the scenery in its name: an impressive coastline, as well as magnificent old-growth redwoods. Joining the redwoods on the wild coastal slope are other big trees—Sitka spruce and Douglas fir.

Steep Damnation Creek Trail plunges through old-growth redwood forest to a hidden rocky beach. Giant ferns, and the pink and purple rhododendron blossoms climbing 30 feet overhead, contribute to the impression that one has strayed into a tropical rain forest.

The Damnation Creek name, as the story goes, was proffered by early settlers who had a devil of a time making their way through the thick forest near the creek banks. Even trailblazer Jedediah Smith, whose expedition camped alongside Damnation Creek in June of 1828, found it very rough going.

The trail's thousand-foot drop to the sea is a challenge and if you trek back up the trail from Damnation Cove on the rare warm day, you might guess some perspiring hiker named the geography around here.

The first 0.5 mile of Damnation Creek Trail gives the hiker contradictory sensory experiences: the sight of the lovely redwood forest vs. the din of Highway 101 traffic.

More pleasant sounds come from the roar of the surf and the foghorn from Crescent City harbor.

DIRECTIONS: From Highway 101 in Crescent City, head 8 miles south to the signed turnout on the coast side of the highway at mile-marker 16.

THE HIKE: The trail soon leaves the sights (but not the sounds) of the highway behind as it climbs through redwood forest for 0.25 mile, crests a ridge, and begins its oceanward descent.

The biggest redwoods come first; in fact, everything looks pretty big up here, including outsized rhododendrons and huge huckleberry bushes. Descend in the footsteps of the native Yurok, who used this trail to reach the beach, where they gathered seaweed and shellfish.

At 0.6 mile, the trail reaches and extends along Coastal Trail (formerly old Highway 101) and traffic noise from modern-day 101 fades away. The redwoods down-slope are smaller but no less handsome and, at about the 1.5-mile mark, Sitka spruce, more tolerant of the salt air, predominate.

Damnation Creek Trail's steep switchbacks lead ever downward. About halfway to the beach, get brief tree-framed views of the Pacific as the trail angles along with Damnation Creek. Wooden bridges facilitate the crossing of two branches of the creek.

Near shore, you'll reach a clifftop perch above the mouth of Damnation Creek. It's an inspiring view: the creek flowing into the surging Pacific, sea stacks and rocky Damnation Cove.

Carefully descend a sketchy trail and rocky stairway to the rocky shore. If it's low tide, you can explore north and south along Damnation Cove. If it's high tide, stay back from the rough surf and relax on higher ground.

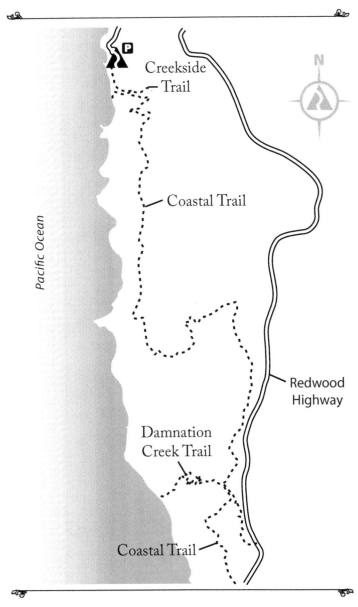

Pacific Ocean

Creekside
Trail

Coastal Trail

Redwood
Highway

Damnation
Creek Trail

Coastal Trail

N

OLD COAST HIGHWAY

LAST CHANCE TRAIL
(CALIFORNIA COASTAL TRAIL)

**To Enderts Beach is 2 miles round trip; to Damnation
Creek Trail junction is 13 miles round trip with 800-foot
elevation gain**

What is now a splendid hiking trail used to be
the Redwood Highway (101). The old highway was
abandoned in 1935 for its present route. This particular length of coastal trail travels over tall coastal
bluffs amidst alder and second-growth redwood then
leads inland to and through old-growth redwoods to
meet Damnation Creek Trail.

Rambling along the old Redwood Highway is
truly a unique hiking experience. Most of the route is
so overgrown by vegetation that it at first seems like
your basic single-track trail; however its highway heritage is obvious when you realize you're hiking along
a fairly flat and wide roadbed—and in places you can
still see the painted centerline on the pavement!

If you just want to see old-growth redwoods, start at the Damnation Creek trailhead (see description) and hike north. Figure on a mellow, more or less level, 10-mile round trip for this redwoods-only hike.

Last Chance Trail is the northernmost stretch of the California Coastal Trail; this is the "last chance" to walk part of the California Coastal Trail (part hiker's dream, part reality) before joining the Oregon Coast Trail.

DIRECTIONS: From Highway 101, about 2 miles south of Crescent City, turn south on Enderts Beach Road and wind 2.5 miles to road's end at Crescent Beach Overlook and the beginning of Last Chance Trail.

THE HIKE: Hike south on the old coast highway and get grand views behind you of the Crescent City coastline. A 0.6-mile descent leads to a three-way junction: a 0.25-mile path leads left along lush, fern-filled Nickel Creek; straight ahead is the southbound Coastal Trail; the right fork continues to Nickel Creek Campground and on to Enderts Beach. The beach is an attractive mixture of boulders, driftwood-strewn shore and a long sand strand.

Enjoy ocean vistas from the level path, which junctions a trail to the beach, then ascends rather steeply via switchbacks. Amidst alder and second-growth redwoods, the old road travels high above the roaring breakers.

Around the 3-mile mark the coastal trail turns
inland and enters old growth. Drama builds as the
redwoods get increasingly grander and the forest
more primeval, particularly when the trail approaches
Damnation Creek.

Cross the creek on a bridge and continue along
the old road, decorated with carpets of moss and
redwood sorrel. Ascend moderately through the
ancient forest while ignoring modernity (traffic noise
from Highway 101) and, about a mile from the creek
crossing, reach the best of the old-growth groves en
route located about 0.5 mile before the junction with
Damnation Creek Trail.

This junction is a good turnaround point unless
you have a car shuttle. From here the trail descends
into thinner redwood forest and leads to Highway 101.

*Ten thousand acres of the redwood forest
primeval preserved in the state park.*

EVERY TRAIL TELLS A STORY.

IV
JEDEDIAH SMITH
REDWOODS SP

HIKE ON.

Fern Falls

Boy Scout Tree

N

Boy Scout Tree Trail

Howland Hill Road

BOY SCOUT TREE
AND FERN FALLS

BOY SCOUT TRAIL

From Howland Hill Road to Fern Falls is 5.6 miles round trip with 300-foot elevation gain

Northernmost of California's redwood state parks, Jedediah Smith beckons the hiker with an impressive redwood forest primeval. The redwood groves, located off the tourist track between Highway 199 and Howland seem splendidly isolated, more so than most of the trees off Highway 101 in RNSP.

This part of the park best honors mountain man/ pathfinder Jedediah Smith, credited with discovering (for west-bound travelers) the Rocky Mountains pass through which most California- and Oregon-bound emigrants traveled.

Goals of this hike are a towering redwood known as Boy Scout Tree and pretty Fern Falls. Boy Scout Trail constructed by the scouts of Crescent City's Troop 10 in the 1930s.

As the story goes, the tree was named because a Boy Scout leader discovered it. Another story has it that the tree took the name of the trail built by the Boy Scouts.

Boy Scout Tree isn't the tallest tree around, but it's a double stem redwood and the two fused trees combine to give it a width of more than 23 feet. (Nearby Girl Scout Tree, discovered in 2018, is also double-stemmed and is about the same width.)

I have fond memories of hiking the trail way back when I was a Boy Scout with Troop 441 from Southern California. It's one of those trails that pulls me back to hike again. I like it for its remote setting (no traffic noise here) and the magnificent old-growth redwood scenery.

It's a diversity of redwood scenery really—lush, fern-filled forest, thinner trees on the ridgetops, denser forest along the creeks. Trees, trees, everywhere. Not that you'd ever get tired of looking at redwoods...but there are some fine specimens of Douglas fir in the 'hood to admire as well.

DIRECTIONS: From Highway 101, at the south end of Crescent City, turn east on Elk Valley Road. After 1.5 miles, fork right on Howland Hill Road and continue east about four more miles to parking for a half-dozen cars and the signed trailhead located on the north side of the road in the tall shadow of redwoods and Douglas fir.

THE HIKE: Stroll the fern-lined path, 300-foot tall trees towering above you. After a mile, the trail follows a redwood-topped ridge, with tall sword ferns pointing the way. At the 1.4-mile mark, descend steps to a footbridge over Jordan Creek. Pass more gigantic trees and descend more steps to another creek and bridged crossing.

After meandering along Jordan Creek, another mile of quiet forest walking brings you to a fork: the right branch goes to Boy Scout Tree while the other leads to Fern Falls, a small cascade at the fringe of a redwood grove.

Three hundred-foot trees tower over the trail.

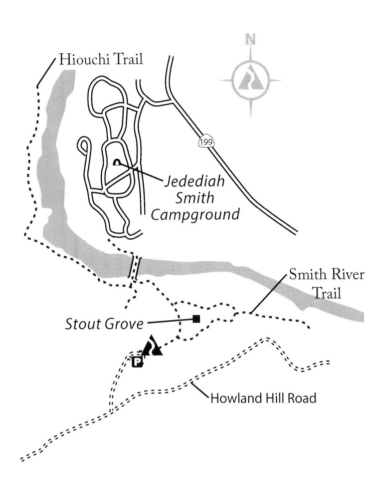

Hiouchi Trail

N

Jedediah
Smith
Campground

199

Smith River
Trail

Stout Grove

Howland Hill Road

STOUT GROVE

STOUT GROVE TRAIL

0.5 mile loop

Many claim Stout Grove in Jedediah Smith Redwoods State Park is the world's most scenic grove of redwoods. And a lot of hikers would agree. There are bigger groves with bigger trees, but none can match its cinematic appeal, a moviemaker's dream.

Begin with the setting: an alluvial flat at the junction of two rivers. Add redwoods, lots of them, and only redwoods—nothing else tall to clutter the forest or detract from the giants. Add a carpet of redwood sorrel and lots of tall sword ferns. An other-worldly setting, to be sure. Not surprisingly, one of the Star Wars series flicks, "Return of the Jedi," was filmed here.

Largest tree in the grove is Stout Tree, distinguished by its rippled bark and 340-foot height. Measuring 20-feet-in-diameter, the tree is indeed stout; however it was named not for its girth but for lumber baron Frank D. Stout. In 1929, Clara Stout donated this 44-acre grove to the Save-the-Redwoods League to preserve it from being logged and to memorialize her husband.

Far from Highway 101 and lightly visited, Stout Grove is a quiet and peaceful place. The grove is fully accessible to those in wheelchairs, and has accessible parking and restrooms. Beyond that, the park service has left well enough alone: no over-the-top signage, displays or interpretive panels.

From Stout Grove, extend your walk by crossing Mill Creek (which flows into the Smith River) to another, smaller redwood grove. In the summer, State Parks installs a footbridge to make it easy for hikers to cross the creek. The Mill Creek footbridge makes it handy to access Hiouchi Trail (see hike description) from Stout Grove.

DIRECTIONS: Howland Hill Road provides year-round access to Stout Grove (and to the trailhead for Hiouchi Trail). From Highway 101 in Crescent City, turn east on Highway 199 and drive 6 miles to Howland Hill Road. Turn right and travel 2 miles to trailhead parking. From Highway 101 south of Crescent City, head east on Elk Valley Road; in a mile when the road forks, bear right. Drive about 6 miles on dirt (and scenic) Howland Hill Road to the Stout Grove parking area.

THE HIKE: From the parking area, descend the paved walkway 100 yards or so to Stout Grove and a little farther to junction the loop trail. Head left, hiking the loop clockwise, and soon reach another junction. The left fork leads to a footbridge over Mill Creek, more redwoods, a (summertime) bridge over the Smith River and the start of Hiouchi Trail.

The right fork is a continuation of the loop trail and extends east along the Smith River. Continue along the loop and turn right at the next junction to return to the trailhead. Alternatively, extend your hike by a mile by walking another 0.5 mile east along the river. Cross pretty Cedar Creek on a footbridge, meander over river bluffs, climb up and down stairs cut into the hillside to reach a good turnaround spot—the junction with Howland Hill Road and Little Bald Hill Trail.

Cross a magic green carpet on the way to Stout Grove.

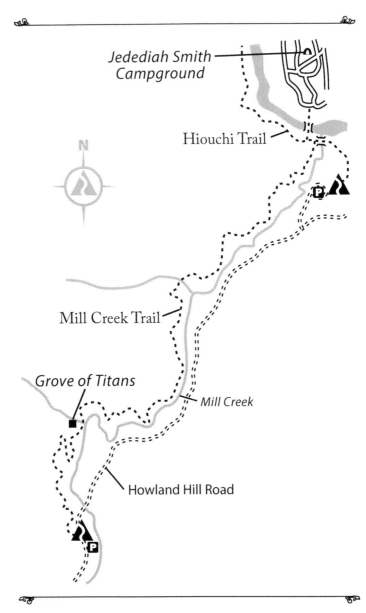

Jedediah Smith
Campground

Hiouchi Trail

Mill Creek Trail

Grove of Titans

Mill Creek

Howland Hill Road

N

GROVE OF TITANS

MILL CREEK TRAIL

To Grove of Titans is 1.7 miles round trip with 200-foot elevation gain; to Smith River is 5.6 miles round trip with 300-foot gain

The massive coastal redwoods that thrive in the heart of Jedediah Smith Redwoods State Park were named Grove of Titans by Humboldt State University researchers who discovered them in the 1990s. Or more accurately re-discovered them because the whereabouts of this forest primeval was known by generations of indigenous people, including the native Tolowa.

As the story goes, the researchers tried to keep the grove a secret—an impossible endeavor given the number of tree-lovers and outdoor adventurers keen on—perhaps obsessed with—finding the world's tallest tree(s). Park officials tried a let's-not-give-out-any-information policy (as did The Trailmaster), but by the time the Titan's GPS coordinates were shared online in 2011 and the grove Google-mapped, the giant tree rush was on.

In retrospect, The Titans were hidden in plain sight—not all that far from Mill Creek Trail. When I read Richard Preston's 2007 book, *The Wild Trees*, I got the impression that the big-tree hunters were making an epic trek through jungle-like terrain.

In their quest to see the Titans, visitors got off the beaten path, trampling understory plants from ferns to fungae, walking roughshod over the redwoods' shallow roots and creating "social trails" (I hate that term), so heavily used they began to resemble official trails.

To protect the trees, park authorities decided to rehab the first mile of Mill Creek Trail and construct a 1,300-foot elevated boardwalk to the Grove of Titans. Mill Creek Trail was rerouted from the edge of the grove to its center so everyone can hike directly to the Titans without needing to go off-trail.

If I didn't know the reason for the new route, I would call the trail "over-engineered" with all those steps and elevated walkways. But in context and, keeping in mind that it will be a popular trail in an increasingly popular national park, let's acknowledge that a narrow footpath of the kind hikers prefer just wouldn't do. And let's give a shout-out to the trail builders for their many months of work and for hand-carrying all that metal infrastructure into the forest.

A little creek, a tributary of Mill Creek, flows across a flat where the smallish (in number of trees) grove lies. Largest tree in the grove, Del Norte Titan

New Trail to the Titans is quite the engineering feat, and surprisingly eco-friendly as well.

towers 307 feet, and ranks as the world's fifth largest coast redwood. (There's a case to be made that it's the largest, based on a "single-stem" measurement.)

The new trail was popular the day it opened in September of 2021 and is becoming more so as word spread about this new easy access to the Titans.

If you want to leave the crowds behind, continue on Mill Creek Trail—it's well worth your time. You'll wander the mossy woodlands on the west side of Mill Creek. Close to the Smith River, at trail's end is a lovely redwood grove.

This is a splendid hike in autumn when the vine and big-leaf maples turn crimson and gold and juicy ripe berries offer a tempting trailside snack.

DIRECTIONS: From Highway 101 in Crescent City, turn east on Elk Valley Road and travel a mile. Turn right on Howland Hill Road and drive about 3.5 miles on the scenic (and partially dirt) road. Look for the signed Mill Creek Trail to the Grove of Titans on your left, opposite a restroom on your right. Park in one of the turnouts along the road.

THE HIKE: Head out on the flat trail amidst the ferns and redwoods. Ascend modest switchbacks then descend near Mill Creek. Walk along a large fallen redwood and shortly thereafter join the wide metal walkway that's elevated to prevent soil compression and let rainfall soak into the soil.

Into the grove we go. The first standout tree is enormous Chesty Puller, two redwoods fused together as one, and supposedly named for a super-buff Marine. Descend metal stairs, cross marshy terrain and reach the main grove. A short detour right leads to a vista point overlooking Mill Creek.

Continue to a second junction where you'll find Lost Monarch, largest single-trunk tree in the grove; at this writing it's ranked as the 5th-largest coast redwood by volume.

The short trail to the left leads to famed double tree, the Screaming Titans and another viewing platform. Back on the main trail, descend past the venerable 1,700-year old El Viejo del Norte redwood. Descend to a creek crossing, where the metal walkway (and the grove) ends. Resume hiking on the now lightly trafficked trail and soon reach Mill Creek. The trail leads briefly along the wide creek then crosses a tributary creek on a footbridge. Narrowing, the path crosses more creeklets, some accompanied by modest-sized redwoods. Get occasional glimpses of Mill Creek meandering along below the trail.

About 2.7 miles out, as the trail approaches the broad Smith River, reach a handsome grove of tall trees, elegantly spaced out on flatland full of ferns, tanoak and small maple trees. From the grove, continue 0.1 to Hiouchi Trail and the gravel bar on the south side of the Smith River. Look across the river toward Stout Grove; if the summer-only footbridge is up, cross the river to the state park campground and more hiking adventures.

If you ever want to feel small, hike to the Grove of Titans!

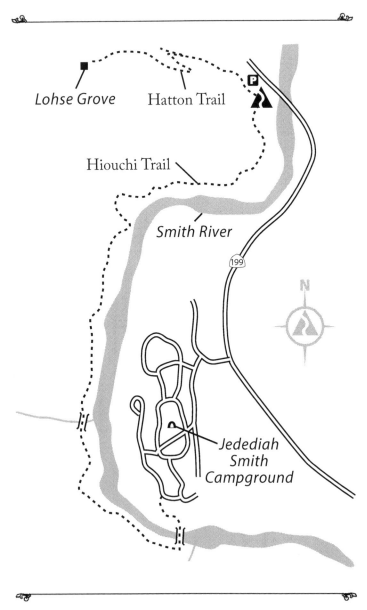

Lohse Grove   Hatton Trail

Hiouchi Trail

Smith River

199

N

Jedediah
Smith
Campground

SMITH RIVER

HIOUCHI TRAIL

From Stout Grove to Hwy 199 is 4 miles round trip with 100-foot elevation gain

Tall trees and a wild river are among the highlights of Hiouchi Trail in Jedediah Smith Redwood State Park. The path extends along the Smith River from Stout Grove to Lohse Grove, located near Highway 199.

From famed Stout Grove, cross Mill Creek on a footbridge (summer-only) or carefully ford the creek in spring and autumn. (In winter or at other times at high water, it's prudent to avoid the creek crossing and begin Hiouchi Trail from its west trailhead, located 4 miles from Crescent City and just before the west end of Hiouchi Bridge on Hwy 199.)

A third option for hiking Hiouchi Trail, and one I really like, is to start this hike from Jedediah Smith Campground and use a footbridge (summer only) over Mill Creek to join the trail.

You'll view pretty pockets of redwoods en route, but the true highlight of this sojourn is hiking along the Smith River. A bonus is the mixed forest at the edge of the old-growth redwoods and along the river: Douglas fir, California bay, tanoak, maple and madrone.

Ah, the Smith River; its un-dammed, wild and free. Anglers love it for its healthy habitat for salmon and steelhead. Hikers love to look at it from Hiouchi Trail, which ascends to the edge of the bluffs in a couple places for grand vistas of the river.

Depending on the light, the Smith River assumes various and stunning shades of green-blue: jade-green, turquoise, teal...well, you be the judge. The river's unique coloration results from up-river deposits of serpentine, a gray-green mineral that's California's official state rock.

DIRECTIONS: Howland Hill Road provides year-round access to Stout Grove (and to the trailhead for Hiouchi Trail). From Highway 101 in Crescent City, turn east on Highway 199 and drive 6 miles to Howland Hill Road. Turn right and travel 2 miles to trailhead parking. From Highway 101 south of Crescent City, head east on Elk Valley Road; in a mile when the road forks, bear right. Drive about 6 miles on dirt (and scenic) Howland Hill Road to the Stout Grove parking area.

THE HIKE: Stroll through Stout Grove and cross Mill Creek (summer footbridge) to join

Hiouchi Trail. If it's redwoods you're looking for, the tall trees come right away: lovely specimens, with a carpet of redwood sorrel beneath them, thriving on an alluvial flat near the river.

The trail dips and rises, offering an occasional view of the Smith River. At about the 1.7-mile mark, the path leads right through a fire-scarred, hollowed-out redwood stump.

Pass an unsigned side trail descending to a beach and ascend toward Highway 199 (you'll hear it before you see it) and reach a junction. The right fork drops to a dirt pullout at the edge of Highway 199 near the large bridge over the Smith River. You can take the left fork about 0.3 mile up a redwood-cloaked ridge to a short path that ascends to the tall trees in Lohse Grove.

A summer-only footbridge over Mill Creek adds to the variety of trails accessible to the hiker.

The Wild Trees: A Story of Passion and Daring by Richard Preston. At great personal risk, daring botanists and amateur naturalists climb to the top of redwoods and discover a lost world, wonders of nature unknown to science.

EVERY TRAIL TELLS A STORY.

Redwood National Park Stories

HIKE ON.

California Coast Trails

Author/naturalist/adventurer Joseph Smeaton Chase
set out in 1911 to take a horseback ride from Mexico to
Oregon along California's multi-splendored coast. He
left us a record of his solo journey in *California Coast
Trails*, a book unequalled before or since as a description of the state's coastline. In this excerpt from his
book, we find Chase reveling in the redwoods, the last
stop on his coast trail, the last pages of *California Coast
Trails*.

As for the redwoods, they were more than ever
memorable in their columnar steadfastness and sym-
metry. A marked habit of the species is its manner
of growing in twins or triplets of stems from a single
base, which in such cases is often of prodigious size.
I noted many trunks that were over twenty feet in
diameter, and many trees that were fully two hundred and fifty feet in height: though by reason of the
colossal size of the whole assembly the dimensions of
individuals would hardly be guessed.

A few maples grew along the creeks, upholstered
completely in the greenest of moss. Their scanty
remaining leaves were glowing with autumn fire, and
the gloom of the forest aisles was lighted up by their
large, ragged stars of purest yellow. On every stump
and fallen log, and on every fork and bulge of living
tree, little elves' gardens of small plants and fungi were
growing—dainty sprays of vaccinium, red and orange
toadstools, barberry, gaultheria: and the roadside

banks were set with myriads of ferns, while the mosses grew to such size that I sometimes mistook them for a young growth of some stiff, heathery plant.

The day was overcast, and all the morning the clouds crept and wreathed about the higher ridges. As the day went on, the fog lowered, till a dense white mist enveloped us and our tree companions. The effect in this close forest was strange and beautiful, the straight, dark stems of the trees standing all about me, outlined against a vaporous background of white that strongly accented the perspective while it obscured every detail. Heavy drops fell from the branches dimly seen overhead, and a low and muffled sound came from the surf on the shore a mile away.

Then for a mile or two I rode through a belt of virgin forest as fine as any I had seen. The redwoods are here almost at their northern boundary, for they appear in Oregon only in one or two scattered groves just beyond the line. It seems remarkable that the tree should cease so abruptly, since it flourishes in undiminished power up to the limits of its range, giving no hint of dissatisfaction with its conditions of soil or climate. California may fairly boast that both species of the greatest American trees, the famous "big tree" and the redwood, are practically confined to the State.

Faith in the Redwoods
John McKinney hiked the length of the California coast and wrote the acclaimed narrative, *Hiking on the Edge: Dreams, Schemes, and 1600 Miles on the California Coastal Trail*. The following is an excerpt from the chapter "Faith in the Redwoods."

Into the rainforest I ramble, amidst moss-draped Sitka spruce and a multitude of skunk cabbage massed on the muddy flats by Skunk Cabbage Creek. The skunk cabbage appears to be a pituitary freak of the plant world, a science experiment gone awry. I spot specimens measuring four feet across, with foot-long leaves, and in the tree-filtered light, the cabbages glow an otherworldly green.

I emerge from lush jungle onto Gold Bluffs Beach, miles of dark, driftwood-strewn sand. After pitching my tent behind a wind barrier of stacked logs, I am soon lulled to sleep by the distant roar of mighty breakers.

Next morning, as I walk a dirt road above the beach, I am surprised to keep company with a wandering herd of Roosevelt elk, more commonly sighted inland grazing the park's prairies. The elk and I part company near Fern Canyon, undoubtedly the most awe-inspiring of the many beautiful "fern canyons" I've hiked along the North Coast. Five-finger, deer, lady, sword and chain ferns smother the high and precipitous walls of the canyon. Bright yellow monkey flowers abound, as well as fairy lanterns, with creamy-white, bell-shaped flowers that hang in clusters.

Having walked through logging and tourist town-ships and through colonnades of redwoods, it occurs to me that here among the ancient trees the only meaningful time distinctions are Now and Forever. Now with its fast-food franchises, drive-through trees and chainsaw sculpture galleries, is sometimes disheartening. Now, in the form of clear-cut land, is even more disheartening.

Forever is the redwoods, whose species name *sempervirens* meaning "everlasting." Although noth-ing in nature lasts forever, the redwood is as close to everlasting as any living thing can get.

One hundred and sixty million years ago, great forests of the tall trees grew in Europe, Asia, and North America. Redwoods towered over the tallest dinosaur. A million or two years ago, with the com-ing of the Ice Age, the redwoods retreated and made a last stand along the northern and central California coast. Ninety-five percent of the world's coast red-woods have been chopped down; four percent are in public ownership.

There's little light on the trail now; it could be any time of day or night. Minutes, hours, and days have little meaning amidst two-thousand-year-old trees and a twenty-million-year-old forest. Hiking among the sorrel and the delicate redwood orchids and straining to see the tops of the trees, I feel the long, joyous evolution of life on earth.

The trail stretches through the great redwood columns toward the rock-bound coast. I could hike here a long time, maybe forever, if my heart doesn't break.

Yurok Creation Story

Salmon, the mighty Klamath River, the redwoods and the elements, including earthquakes, are integral to Yurok identity going all the way back to their earliest stories. Below is a paraphrased and condensed version of the Yurok creation story from *River of Renewal: Myth and History in the Klamath Basin* by Stephen Most.

In the beginning of time, the Creator came to the mouth of the Klamath. He stood on the beach and thought: "This is a great river. I want to leave my children here. But there's nothing for them to eat." So the Creator called to the spirit of the river, Pulekukwerek.... Pulekukwerek answered, "I can feed them. I can send fish"....Greatest of all, Nepewo entered the river each fall, leading the salmon people. Then the river spirit made human people.

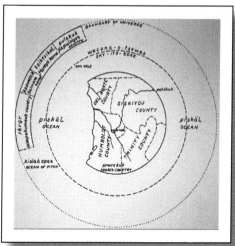

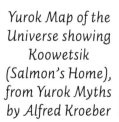

Yurok Map of the Universe showing Koowetsik (Salmon's Home), from Yurok Myths by Alfred Kroeber

Death Valley NP
YOSEMITE NATIONAL PARK
LAVA BEDS NM
Yosemite National Park
Pinnacles NP
Joshua Tree National Park
EUGENE O'NEILL NHS
Pinnacles NP
Whiskeytown-Shasta Trinity NRA
Cabrillo NM
Golden Gate National Recreation Area
REDWOOD NP
DEVILS POSTPILE NM
LASSEN VOLCANIC NATIONAL PARK
CHANNEL ISLANDS NATIONAL PARK
Cabrillo NM
LAVA BEDS NM
Joshua Tree National Park
MOJAVE NPRES
MUIR WOODS NM
César Chávez NM
LASSEN VOLCANIC NATIONAL PARK
Rosie the Riveter NHS
YOSEMITE NATIONAL PARK
John Muir NHS
Santa Monica Mountains NRA
MOJAVE NPRES
Death Valley NP
Cabrillo NM
Pinnacles NP
Death Valley NP
POINT REYES NS
SEQUOIA–KINGS CANYON NATIONAL PARKS
EUGENE O'NEILL NHS
CHANNEL ISLANDS NATIONAL PARK
REDWOOD NP
DEVILS POSTPILE NM
POINT REYES NS

CALIFORNIA'S NATIONAL PARKS

Other states have national parks with tall trees, high peaks, deep canyons, long seashores and vast deserts, but only California can claim all these grand landscapes within its boundaries.

California boasts nine national parks, the most in the nation. In addition, the state's national parklands include national recreation areas, national monuments, national historic parks, a national seashore and a national preserve.

The state features one of America's oldest national parks—Yosemite set aside in 1890—and one of its newest—César E. Chávez National Monument established in 2012.

Mere acreage does not a national park make, but California's national parks include the largest park in the contiguous U.S.—3.3-million acre Death Valley National Park. Yosemite (748,542 acres) and Joshua Tree (790,636 acres) are also huge by any park standards. Even such smaller parklands as Redwoods National Park and Pt. Reyes National Seashore are by no means small.

California and The National Park Idea

Not long after John Muir walked through Mariposa Grove and into the Yosemite Valley, California's natural treasures attracted attention worldwide and conservationists rallied to preserve them as parks. As the great naturalist put it in 1898: "Thousands of nerve-shaken, overcivilized people are beginning to find out that going to the mountains is going home; that wilderness is a necessity; and that mountain parks and reservations are useful not only as fountains of timber and irrigating rivers, but as fountains of life."

The National Park Service, founded in 1916, was initially guided by borax tycoon-turned-park-champion Stephen T. Mather and his young assistant, California attorney Horace Albright. The park service's mission was the preservation of "the scenery and the natural and historic objects and the wild life" and the provision "for the enjoyment of the same in such manner and by such means as will leave them unimpaired for the enjoyment of future generations."

The invention of the automobile revolutionized national park visitation, particularly in car-conscious California. John Muir called them "blunt-nosed mechanical beetles," yet as one California senator pointed out, "If Jesus Christ had an automobile he wouldn't have ridden a jackass into Jerusalem."

With cars came trailers, and with trailer camps came concessionaires. National parks filled with mobile cities of canvas and aluminum, and by visitors anxious to see California's natural wonders. During the 1920s and 30s, the park service constructed signs identifying scenic features and rangers assumed the role of interpreting nature for visitors.

By 1930 California had four national parks: Yosemite, Lassen, Sequoia and General Grant (Kings Canyon.) In the 1930s, two big desert areas—Joshua Tree and Death Valley—became national monuments.

With the 1960s came hotly contested, and eventually successful campaigns to create Redwood National

Steven Mather (R) and his assistant Horace Albright guided the National Park Service in its early days.

Park and Point Reyes National Seashore. During the
1970s the National Park Service established parks near
the state's big cities—Golden Gate National Recreation Area on the San Francisco waterfront and Marin
headlands and Santa Monica Mountains National
Recreation Area, a Mediterranean ecosystem near
Los Angeles. Also during that decade, Mineral King
Valley was saved from a mega-ski resort development
and added to Sequoia National Park. Channel Islands
National Park, an archipelago offshore from Santa
Barbara, was established in 1980.

During the 1980s and 1990s, major conservation battles raged in the desert. After more than two
decades of wrangling, Joshua Tree and Death Valley
national monuments were greatly expanded and given
national park status, and the 1.6-million acre Mojave
National Preserve was established under provisions of
the 1994 California Desert Conservation Act.

Today, the National Park Service must address
challenging questions: How best to regulate concessionaires? Should motor vehicles be banned from
Yosemite Valley? How can aging park facilities cope
with many years of deferred maintenance?

And the biggest issue of all: How will our parks
(indeed our planet!) cope with the rapidly increasing
effects of climate change?

The consequences of climate change to California's national parks is ever more apparent. In recent

years, after prolonged droughts, devastating wildfires burned the Yosemite backcountry, parts of Sequoia National Park and more than half the Santa Monica Mountains National Recreation Area. Scientists have discovered that trees in Sequoia and Kings Canyon national parks endure the worst ozone levels of all national parks, in part because of their proximity to farm-belt air in the San Joaquin Valley.

California's national parklands struggle with an ever-increasing numbers of visitors. The California Office of Tourism charts visitation to national parks along with airports, hotel occupancy and other attractions such as Disneyland and Universal Studios. Yosemite is California's most-visited park with 4.5 to 5 million visitors a year, and many other parks count millions of visitors or "visitor days," per year.

What may be the saving grace of national parks is the deep-seated, multi-generational pride Americans have for their national parklands. We not only love national parks, we love the very idea of national parks. Even in an era of public mistrust toward government, national parks remain one of the most beloved institutions of American life.

National Parks have often been celebrated as America's best idea. As writer Wallace Stegner put it: "National parks are the best idea we ever had. Absolutely American, absolutely democratic, they reflect us at our best rather than our worst."

The Trails

The state of the state's national park trail system is excellent. Trailhead parking, interpretive panels and displays, as well as signage, is generally tops in the field. Backcountry junctions are usually signed and trail conditions, with a few exceptions of course, range from good to excellent.

Trail systems evolved on a park-by-park basis and it's difficult to speak in generalities about their respective origins. A good deal of Yosemite's trail system was in place before the early horseless carriages chugged into the park.

Several national parks were aided greatly by the Depression-era Civilian Conservation Corps of the 1930s. Sequoia and Pinnacles national parks, for example, have hand-built trails by the CCC that are true gems, highlighted by stonework and bridges that would no doubt be prohibitively expensive to construct today.

Scout troops, the hard-working young men and women of the California Conservation Corps and many volunteer groups are among the organizations that help park staff build and maintain trails.

The trail system in California's national parklands shares many characteristics in common with pathways overseen by other governmental bodies, and have unique qualities as well. One major difference between national parks and, for example, California's state parks, is the amount of land preserved as wilderness. A majority of Yosemite, Sequoia, Death Valley, Joshua Tree and several more parks are official federally designated wilderness. Wilderness comprises some 94 percent of Yosemite National Park, 93 percent of Death Valley National Park, and more than 80 percent of Joshua Tree National Park.

On national park maps you'll find wilderness areas delineated as simply "Wilderness." Unlike the Forest Service, the Bureau of Land Management or other wilderness stewards, the National Park Service does not name its wilderness areas.

Author John McKinney admires the sign for Yosemite's Four Mile Trail.

"Wilderness" is more than a name for a wild area. By law, a wilderness is restricted to non-motorized entry—that is to say, equestrian and foot travel. Happily, hikers do not have to share the trails with snowmobiles or mountain bikes in national park wilderness.

Because national park trails attract visitors from all over the globe, the park service makes use of international symbols on its signage, and the metric system as well. Don't be surprised if you spot trail signs with distance expressed in kilometers as well as miles and elevation noted in meters as well as feet.

The hikers you meet on a national park trail may be different from the company you keep on trails near home. California's national parks attract increasing numbers of ethnically and culturally diverse hikers of all ages, shapes and sizes, from across the nation and around the world. Once I counted ten languages on a popular trail in Yosemite! The hiking experience is much enriched by sharing the trail with hikers from literally all walks of life.

CALIFORNIA'S NATIONAL PARKLANDS

Alcatraz Island
Cabrillo National Monument
Castle Mountains National Monument
César E. Chávez National Monument
Channel Islands National Park
Death Valley National Park
Devils Postpile National Monument
Eugene O'Neill National Historic Site
Fort Point National Historic Site
Golden Gate National Recreation Area
John Muir National Historic Site
Joshua Tree National Park
Lassen Volcanic National Park
Lava Beds National Monument
Manzanar National Historic Site
Mojave National Preserve
Muir Woods National Monument
Pinnacles National Park
Point Reyes National Seashore
Port Chicago Naval Magazine National Memorial
Presidio of San Francisco
Redwood National and State Parks
Rosie the Riveter WWII Home Front National
    Historic Park
San Francisco Maritime National Historic Park
Santa Monica Mountains National Recreation Area
Sequoia and Kings Canyon National Parks
Tule Lake National Monument
Whiskeytown National Recreation Area
Yosemite National Park

The Hiker's Index

Celebrating the Scenic, Sublime and Sensational Points of Interest in California's National Parks

State with the most National Parks

California, with 9

Largest National Park in Contiguous U.S.

Death Valley with 3.3 million acres

Third Largest National Park in Contiguous U.S.

Mojave National Preserve

Foggiest Place on the West Coast

Point Reyes Lighthouse, Point Reyes National Seashore

World's Tallest Tree

A 379.7-foot high coast redwood named Hyperion in Redwood National Park

World's Largest Tree

General Sherman Tree, 275 feet tall, with a base circumference of 102 feet, growing in the Giant Forest Area of Sequoia National Park

World's Largest-In-Diameter Tree

General Grant Tree, dubbed "the nation's Christmas tree," more than 40 feet in diameter at its base, growing in Kings Canyon National Park.

Largest Elephant Seal Population on Earth

San Miguel Island, Channel Islands National Park

Highest Point in Contiguous U.S.

Mt. Whitney (14,508 feet in elevation) on the far eastern boundary of Sequoia National Park

Lowest Point in Western Hemisphere

Badwater (282 feet below sea level) in Death Valley National Park

California's Largest Island

Santa Cruz Island, Channel Islands National Park

Only Major Metropolis Bisected by a Mountain Range

Los Angeles, by the Santa Monica Mountains (National Recreation Area)

Highest Waterfall in North America

Yosemite Falls, at 2,425 feet, in Yosemite National Park

JOHN MCKINNEY

John McKinney is an award-winning writer, public speaker, and author of 30 hiking-themed books: inspiring narratives, top-selling guides, books for children.

John is particularly passionate about sharing the stories of California trails. He is the only one to have visited—and written about—all 280 California State Parks. John tells the story of his epic hike along the entire California coast in the critically acclaimed *Hiking on the Edge: Dreams, Schemes, and 1600 Miles on the California Coastal Trail.*

For 18 years John, aka The Trailmaster, wrote a weekly hiking column for the Los Angeles Times, and has hiked and enthusiastically told the story of more than 10 thousand miles of trail across California and around the world. His "Every Trail Tells a Story" series of guides highlight the very best hikes in California.

The intrepid Eagle Scout has written more than a thousand stories and opinion pieces about hiking, parklands, and our relationship with nature.

A passionate advocate for hiking and our need to reconnect with nature, John is a frequent public speaker, and shares his tales on radio, on video, and online.

JOHN MCKINNEY:
"EVERY TRAIL TELLS A STORY."

HIKE ON.

TheTrailmaster.com

Made in the USA
Monee, IL
09 June 2022

97720100R00085